The Heart of Friends:
Quaker History and Beliefs

By Glenn W. Leppert

With contributions by
David W. Kingrey

Barclay College
PUBLISHERS

Glenn Leppert

Barclay College Publishers
607 N. Kingman St.
Haviland, KS 67059

Publisher's Cataloging-in-Publication data

Names: Leppert, Glenn W., author. |
Kingrey, David W., contributor.
Title: Heart of Friends : Quaker history and beliefs /
Glenn W. Leppert; with contributions by David W. Kingrey.
Description: Includes bibliographical references and index. |
Haviland, KS: Barclay College Publishers, 2020.
Identifiers: ISBN: 978-1-7354646-0-2
Subjects: LCSH Society of Friends. | Quakers--History. | BISAC
RELIGION / Christianity / Quaker | RELIGION / History
Classification: LCC BX7731.3 .L47 2020 | DDC 289.6--dc23

ISBN: 978-1-7354646-0-2

ENDORSEMENTS

Many books have been written over the years that have attempted to chronicle the growth and development of the Friends movement, but very few have approached the topic from a distinctively and unapologetically evangelical perspective. The Heart of Friends seeks to remedy this situation. To borrow from Elton Trueblood's comments on a similar effort that was made during the previous century, "this book represents what is probably the majority of living Quakers, those with a frankly evangelical mood." It is with deep gratitude and great joy that I welcome this fresh treatment of Quaker history and theology for a new generation of Evangelical Friends.

David O. Williams, D.Min., George Fox Seminary (Portland Seminary)

Friends, Glenn Leppert and David Kingrey have given us a thoughtful, accessible, and generous overview of Quakerism today. Wide-ranging and appropriately international in scope, The Heart of Friends looks at Quakerism from an evangelical perspective, but acknowledges the diversity of the contemporary Quaker world and is fair to all persuasions of Friends. This is a welcome and useful work.

Thomas D. Hamm, Ph.D., Indiana University

"The Heart of Friends; Quaker History and Beliefs" maintains a consistent level of excellence in capturing and communicating the essential history and beliefs of true Quakerism. The scholarship and critical analysis of the authors provide a treatise that is academic and appropriate for use as a textbook in Quaker colleges and graduate schools worldwide. Also, through skillful writing, the

book is suitable for individuals and church groups with subsequent discussion questions and suggested projects designed to enrich the participant's learning experience and provide practical application of the content. Readers of this book will encounter the fullness of the Friends movement and a framework for individual and group formation into Christ-likeness while being stimulated to be instruments of global transformation for the glory of God. It is a must-read for every lifelong learner!

Adrian Halverstadt, Ph.D., Trinity/University of Liverpool

Glenn Leppert and David Kingrey have done it! They have put the pieces of George Fox and Margaret Fell back together again. They have shown that the early Friends vision of Christian wholeness, in which mysticism (cultivation of the inner life), evangelism, cutting-edge social action, and dynamic messages all belong together. Any person seeking faith, who wants to get it all together, needs to read this book.

Jack Kirk, M.Div., Christian Theological Seminary

Glenn Leppert has made a welcome contribution to Quaker literature in his book titled, "The Heart of Friends; Quaker History and Beliefs." This [book], though short, gives a good and extensively- documented outline of both Quaker history and beliefs. The extensive footnotes and the bibliographies for further study at the end of each chapter will allow the reader to delve deeper into the details of Quaker history and beliefs. Leppert does a good job of putting the history into the context of general church history with several timelines. Other appealing factors of the book are the side bars with brief biographical sketches, and the excellent lists of "Discussion Questions/Projects" at the end of each chapter. These Discussion Questions/Projects will allow a teacher using this book

as a text to enhance the class with thoughtful assignments.
D. Gene Pickard, D.Miss., Trinity Evangelical Divinity School

In The Heart of Friends, Glenn Leppert and Dave Kingrey fill an essential gap in Friends scholarship – a contemporary history of Quakerism from a Christian perspective. Academically rigorous and historically comprehensive, while still an accessible and entertaining read, it is a must-have for scholars, pastors, students, or anyone else seeking to understand the Christian foundation and heartbeat of Quakerism.
Derek Brown, Ph.D., Johnson University

You are my friends if you do what I command. I no longer call you servants, because a servant does not know his master's business. Instead, I have called you friends, for everything that I learned from my Father I have made known to you.
John 15:14-15

DEDICATION

For Sue, friend and companion in our journey together among Friends for the past fifty years. -Glenn W. Leppert

For Carol, David, and Scott and their families. -David W. Kingrey

TABLE OF CONTENTS

ACKNOWLEDGMENTS

I suspect no writing is ever done truly alone. There are authors whose works need to be consulted and colleagues with whom to discuss ideas. That certainly has been true of this writing. It was Dave Kingrey, a fellow professor here at Barclay College, who sparked the idea and gave encouragement along the way. I owe much to the books and articles that he passed onto me. Without his sharp eye and keen understanding of grammar and form that he applied to the work; it would not be near what it now is. Here I wish to recognize his contribution to this book.

I would like as well to acknowledge colleagues who helped with ideas and with material. Jeannie Ross, librarian at Barclay College, helped locate volumes. Derek Brown, Barclay professor, critiqued portions of chapters. Royce Frazier, college president, gave encouragement. I would especially like to thank Paul Anderson, scholar, for the foreword. Thanks also go to Thomas D. Hamm, Quaker historian; Jack Kirk, Friends pastor; Gene Pickard, former missionary and professor; Adrian Halverstadt, EFCI-NA director; and David Williams, Lead Superintendent of Mid-America Yearly Meeting, for their evaluative comments.

A very special thanks also to Rachel Mortimer for her efforts moving this from a manuscript to a finished book.

Glenn W. Leppert

FOREWORD

The body of Christ is a unity, but its strength lies in the power and complementarity of its various members. That being the case, it behooves each part of the body to understand its calling well and to live fully into its role in furthering the work of Christ the head. This can only happen, though, if members of each group understand their roles, and illuminating that vocation is what this book furthers so well.

While the Quaker movement is a relatively small part of the larger Christian movement, numbering less than half a million, it has had a disproportionately large impact on world history and societal ethos. As one of the first evangelistic campaigns in the Puritan era, the Valiant Sixty spread the news locally and abroad that Christ is come to teach his people himself. As Quakers got involved in business, trade, and industry; they did so with honesty and integrity. That also explains some of their impressive success. Quakers made huge impacts in the fields of science, technology, banking, education, medicine, and social work—challenging slavery, violence, and injustice. As champions of women's rights, civil rights, and economic reforms, Quakers have long endeavored for the prayer of Jesus to be answered: that God's will would be carried out on earth as it is in heaven.

In these and other ways, Friends have embraced the biblical vision of a realized eschatology. God's kingdom-leadership is available here and now, if we will but attend, discern, and mind the present leadership of the Resurrected Lord. That dynamic reality happens best, though, as we learn more about how Christ has led in the past, piquing our sensitivity to how he might be leading in the present, through the truth-unveiling and power-inspiring work of the Holy

Spirit. In helping us appreciate more fully the history and beliefs of Christ-centered Friends, that is what this book aspires to facilitate.

As you read this book, allow the inspiration of how Christ has led in the past to open today's hearts and minds to how he might be leading today. And, as Glenn Leppert, Dave Kingrey, and others have reminded us, we too are part of that never-ending story, as we embrace the heart of the people called Quakers, seeking to become genuine friends of Jesus, as we seek to be receptive and responsive to his present leadings. The manna falls from heaven on a daily basis, and only in its daily gathering is it fully sustaining.

Paul Anderson
Professor of Biblical and Quaker Studies
George Fox University

PREFACE

The Friends, also known as Quakers, have a rich and brilliant history. They have made a vital witness to values that are greatly needed in our twenty-first century: simplicity, integrity, equality, peace, education, missions, community, and stewardship. Since the beginning of the Quaker movement in the seventeenth century to the present, Quakers have labored steadfastly, and many have sacrificed their lives, to enrich the lives of others. John Woolman (1720-1772) expressed eloquently this high goal. "To turn all the treasures we possess into the channel of universal love becomes the business of our lives . . . To labor for a perfect redemption from this spirit of oppression is the business of the whole family of Christ Jesus in this world" (1763).

In the spirit of liberation, the "Holy Experiment" of William Penn (1644-1718) in Pennsylvania gave freedom of belief and equality to all citizens, and prisons were transformed into educational institutions. Many of the principles of the Pennsylvania government became foundational to the United States Constitution. William Penn's vision of a Union of Nations was the forerunner of the United Nations. With commitment equal to that of Woolman and Penn, Elizabeth Gurney Fry (1780-1845) dedicated her life to the reform of the Newgate prison in England where the conditions were horrendous. Many of the reform measures she instituted set the standard for humanitarian treatment of prisoners in American prisons. Of further note, is the significance of the work of Laura Haviland (1808-1898), who with Charles, her husband, founded the Raisin Institute in Raisin, Michigan, which was a school for indigent children. It was one of the first in America to allow African Americans to attend.

With all their admirable achievements, Quakers have also made costly mistakes, some of which have led to disunity. It is important that these blemishes be acknowledged because we can grow from our mistakes. The weaknesses, as well as the strengths, of Quakers are discussed in this book.

Glenn Leppert, a lifelong Quaker, whose doctoral studies were in history, has devoted his life to writing and to Friends education internationally. In *The Heart of Friends; Quaker History and Beliefs*, Glenn has clearly captured the heart of Friends, in their beliefs and throughout their history. He has demonstrated that Quakerism is not merely a historical movement, but a live option for persons, who are thirsting for an abundant life of self-giving love, to help make the abundant life promised by Jesus in John 10:10 available to others. His promise is, "I have come that they may have life, and have it to the full."

Through the centuries of challenges and successes, the high aspiration of Quakers, who have been known for quaking in the presence and "the power of the Lord," is faithfulness to the teaching of Jesus in John 15:14, the Scripture passage from which the name, Friends, came, "You are my friends if you do what I command."

David Kingrey
Barclay College
2020

Glenn Leppert

1
Antecedents

4 BC to AD 590 the Apostolic Church (Ancient Period)
591 to 1517 the Medieval Church (Medieval Period)
1517 to present the Modern Church (Modern Period)
1374 founding of *Devotio Moderna*
1387 the Brethren of the Common Life founded in Holland
1517 the Protestant Reformation
1519 Ulrich Zwingli begins the Swiss Reformation.
1520 the beginning of the Anabaptist movement
1525 William Tyndale's New Testament translation
1530 the Augsburg Confession
1534 the Acts of Supremacy
1541 John Knox leads reformation in Scotland.
1559 Elizabethan Prayer Book published

Religious confusion prevailed in England from 1534, when the Acts of Supremacy made King Henry VIII the head of the church, until well into the seventeenth century.[1] The reformation that took place in England under Henry VIII, Edward VI, and Elizabeth was organized and efficient but did not result in a spiritual church.[2] With no spiritual leader the church in England became "a communion halfway between evangelical Protestantism and Roman Catholicism"[3] and being neither, gave rise to much conflict and uncertainty. By the seventeenth century, as Margaret Bacon reminds us,

---

[1] Rufus Jones, *George Fox: Seeker and Friend* (New York: Harper and Brothers Publishers, 1930), 4.

[2] Ibid. 4.

[3] Lars Qualben, *A History of the Christian Church* (New York: Thomas Nelson

"England was a bubbling cauldron of religious controversy."[4] There was no spiritual leader to gather the people to truth.

By the time of the English Civil War (1642-1651) there were numerous groups and movements all across England.[5] There were those known as the Levellers led by one John Lilburne who advocated complete religious freedom.[6] There were the Fifth Monarchy Men looking for an immediate return of the Lord and the inauguration of his kingdom of saints.[7] There were many others, not so organized as the Levellers and the Fifth Monarchists, known simply as Seekers. These men and women were searching for spiritual truth. Those within this category were also known as Baptists, Ranters, and Separatists. They believed that the Roman Catholic Church was corrupt and that the Church of England, and the various Puritan bodies, the Presbyterians, and Congregationalists offered no spiritual help.[8] Along with these were the Friends of Truth, also known as the Quakers.[9] To understand this situation in England in the mid-seventeenth century we would profit by a brief overview of Church History with a focused look at what transpired in England.

1958), 318.

[4] Margaret Bacon, *The Quiet Rebels: The Story of the Quakers in America* (New York: Basic Books, 1969), 9.

[5] Kenneth Scott Latourette, *A History of Christianity.* (New York: Harper and Row, 1953), 821.

[6] John Simpkin, "The Levelers," Retrieved from https://spartacus-educational.com/STUlevellers.htm. John Lilburne believed: "No man should be punished or persecuted . . . for preaching or publishing his opinion on religion."

[7] Latourette, 822.

[8] *Encyclopedia Britannica Online,* s.v. "Seeker."

[9] The situation was much as it is today, with people looking to cults and Eastern religions to find meaning for life.

The history of the church may be divided into three distinctive periods. The first, or Ancient Period, covers the years from the time of Jesus Christ to the age of Gregory the Great in 590. This Ancient Period was followed by a Medieval Period running from Gregory to Martin Luther and the outbreak of the Reformation in 1517. The third period is the Modern Period from the Reformation to the present. George Fox and the beginnings of the Friends Movement (Quakers) fit into the very early portion of the third, or Modern Period. The Friends movement began one hundred-seven years after the outbreak of the Reformation.

The Ancient Period saw the beginnings of the church. Following the outpouring of the Holy Spirit at Pentecost the apostles and other disciples were as Jesus had said, "witnesses in Jerusalem and in all Judea and Samaria, and to the ends of the earth" (Acts 1:8). They took the gospel everywhere. As they did, they established congregations in all parts of the Roman Empire and created practices related to life, worship, and organization. Brotherly love, working together in community, simple informal worship with hymns and prayers and Scripture reading marked their time together. Two sacraments were observed: the Lord's Supper (communion) and baptism. They believed Christ was the son of God; that he was crucified, buried, and raised on the third day; and that through his resurrection were available to all who believed, salvation by faith, and the possibility of a consecrated, sanctified life.

As the New Testament Church grew and spread across the world it also began to change. Some of this change was simply the church learning to take a stand.[10] Early persecution strengthened the

---

[10] Ian Shaw, *Christianity: The Biography: 2,000 years of Global History* (Grand Rapids: Zondervan, 2016), 53.

testimony of the church and scattered it around the world. Persecution also engendered the writings, both the apologies (defenses) and the reasoned theologies to encourage and to teach.[11] As Christianity became accepted in the Roman world and persecution ended, the church increased efforts at missions and delved deeper in expounding theological concepts. In this time the church was faced with increased need to combat heresy and dissension.

About the year 500 A.D. the Roman Empire collapsed and the Church found herself in the position of holding what had been the great empire together. The need to convert and to teach the many barbarian tribes who had infiltrated the Roman Empire and to deal with the false ideas that these people brought to Christianity forced the Church to adopt new administrative skills.

By the beginning of the Medieval Period leadership (administrative) of the church was beginning to be concentrated in Rome under the Bishop of Rome. The Bishop there claimed to be and was acknowledged to be the spiritual and physical leader of the church and as such began to accumulate power.[12] The first one in this position to consolidate that power and to expand it was Gregory I, known also as Gregory the Great. Serving in a time of widespread political confusion (540-604) he used his influence to bring about a stable political situation. Gregory never called himself Pope, but his

---

[11] An apology is a defense of a particular theology or set of beliefs. Christian writers like Justin Martyr, Tatian, and Tertullian wrote to defend Christianity against a variety of charges. The reasoned theologies came later with works by Clement, Origin, Augustine, and John Chrysostom.

[12] Howard Vos, *Highlights of Church History* (Chicago: Moody Press, 1960), 47. It was Ignatius, bishop of Antioch, around about 110 who began to teach that elders were to obey the bishop and that the bishop over any region had supremacy over any local church.

consolidation of power and his strategic use of that power became the basis for the medieval papacy. Sometime early in the sixth century the bishop in Rome became known as "pope" meaning "poppa" or father.

The popes began to influence church traditions dictating matters of worship: order, language, the music that could be used. All matters of thought, whether praxis or theology, came under the influence of the pope. In fact, all matters of polity and policy were controlled by and through the pope. And through the papacy there came to be many additions to what had marked the early church.

Church historian Lars Qualben wrote:

> A desire for more specific order, and a pressing demand for proper safeguards against heresy resulted in a gradual transfer of the preaching, teaching, and the administration of the Sacraments from the gifted men to the local elders . . . The official function was now performed by elders only. The ministry of the Word and the Sacraments became official, and marked the beginning of the division of Christianity into "clergy" (chosen ones) and "laity" (the masses).[13]

Whereas the Apostolic Church was well described by the New Testament itself: "For where two or three gather in my name, there am I with them"(Mt. 18:20), the Medieval Church came to be best described by something far more complicated: "Where the Bishop in Apostolic succession is, there is the church. Outside of this there

---

[13] Qualben, 94.

is no salvation."[14]

Medieval theologians seemed uncertain how to sort out Scripture from tradition. Whereas the early Ecumenical church councils had invariably settled matters on the basis of Scripture, theology in the Middle Ages began to treat church tradition and ecclesiastical authority as the same as the Word of God.

In the fourteenth and fifteenth centuries, what one historian calls "shadows," began to appear across wide areas of Western Europe. That historian writes:

> The vigorous expansion into bordering areas that had marked European history since the eleventh century came to an end. The Christian West fought to halt the expansion of the Muslim Turks but did not completely succeed. Plague, famine, and recurrent wars decimated populations and snuffed out their former prosperity. The papacy and feudal governments struggled against mounting institutional chaos. Powerful mystical and heretical movements and new critical currents in Scholasticism rocked the established religious and philosophical equilibrium."[15]

Thus, the fourteenth and fifteenth centuries were centuries of change. Politically, nation states were rising. Intellectually, the

---

[14] Saint Cyprian of Carthage in the third century may have been the first to state *extra ecclesiam nulla salus* which means "outside the Church there is no salvation." By the time of the late Medieval Period it was also understood that the church was the only valid succession of spiritual authority.

[15] Mortimer Chambers, et. al., *The Western Experience*, 4th ed. (New York: Alfred A. Knopf, 1987), 390.

Renaissance had come to full bloom. Religiously, the Catholic Church was in a state of decay. "Negligence, ignorance, absenteeism, and sexual immorality were widespread among the clergy and taken for granted by the people."[16] Culturally and economically, everything was in flux. Yet, while the world was quickly changing, the church was not. "Everywhere in the world new life was stirring," says Reformation historian William Stevenson, "in every direction there was progress, advance, and enlightenment; in every branch and department of life men were reaching forward—in all except one only, the church of Christ."[17]

There were attempts to change, to renew the church, well before the Reformation. In 1378 for example, in a book, *Of Civil Dominion*, John Wycliffe pled for the removal of immoral clergymen and a reduction of church properties which he saw as a source of corruption.[18] Beginning in 1379, Wycliffe openly began to oppose the dogma of the church and attacked the papacy. To counter the teaching of the church he began to make the Bible available to common folk in their own tongue. John Hus began to preach reform in Bohemia about 1409. Another major figure demanding reform was Girolamo Savonarola, a Dominican monk who denounced clerical corruption, despotic rule, and the exploitation of the poor. Hus and Savonarola were silenced by the Church; Hus was burned at the stake, and Savonarola was hanged.

---

[16] Philip McNair, "Seeds of Renewal" in Tom Dowley, ed, *Introduction to the History of Christianity* (Minneapolis: Fortress Press, 2002), 352.

[17] William Stevenson, *The Story of the Reformation* (Louisville: John Knox Press, 1959), 15.

[18] Earle E. Cairns, *Christianity Through the Centuries* (Grand Rapids: Zondervan, 1996), 244.

From within the Church there were also reforming attempts. A series of Reforming Councils met from 1409 to 1449. These councils were called specifically to end the Great Schism, which began in 1378, and saw two different popes chosen by the College of Cardinals. The Council of Pisa (1409), the Council of Constance (1414-1418), the Councils of Basel and Florence (1431-1449) met and declared that the Church Council and not the pope was the highest authority in the Church, but were never able to enact this concept. Other than ending the schism, the councils had little impact on change in the Church.

Other attempts at change came through spiritual revival among the people. In the late fourteenth century, a movement known as *Devotio Moderna* ("the modern way of serving God") began in northern Europe.[19] The movement emphasized personal devotion and involvement in society. From this revival came others. One other was the creation of the Brethren of the Common Life in 1387 which, as it spread across Europe, prepared the hearts of people for the change that eventually came.[20]

But, by 1517, it seemed impossible that change could be made. "Never had official religion been at lower ebb, or the public image of Christianity more defaced," states Philip McNair, "than in the second decade of the sixteenth century. It seemed as though all opposition to the unreformed Catholic Church from within and without was dying away."[21]

But change did come and in 1517 the change, the Reformation, caused the church to be torn into two opposing camps with

---

[19] McNair, "Seeds of Renewal," 359.

[20] Ibid., p. 361.

[21] Ibid., p. 365.

tradition and many questionable practices on the one hand and new thoughts and purposes for the church by the reformers on the other.

Still, the Catholic Church clung to the many traditions and practices that she had created for herself and which she was not willing to let go. Over the years, but especially from the beginning of the Medieval Period, the church had added to the original gospel message and had made the plan and process of salvation much more complicated. Instead of Christ as the mediator of the new covenant connecting God and humankind with salvation through the act of faith, the Church now had an elaborate scheme that included a special priesthood, bishops, several sacraments, the Virgin Mary, and other saints, as a hierarchy separating humankind and God.

The reformed churches could not agree on what traditions were valid to maintain and which were definitely to be rejected. What was the correct understanding of the church, the role of the church? What involvement did humankind have in the process of salvation? How were baptism, communion, and church membership to be handled? What was a correct understanding of salvation, redemption, justification, and sanctification?

While these questions were universal and everywhere men and women wrestled with possible answers, these questions were much debated in England. What was the correct stance for the church? Henry VIII had moved the church out of Roman Catholicism and made it a national church. This was not because he wanted to adopt a Protestant worldview, but rather because he wanted a church that would approve his need for a divorce. With the change, people were uncertain whether they were Roman Catholic or

Protestant.[22] Further the move away from Catholicism was made because of politics and the political and social situation of the country was fragmented—a social revolution was in process, evicted tenants and monks from the closed monasteries wandered aimlessly across the land, the treasury was empty, the nation was in debt, prestige and influence abroad were waning, agricultural efforts were failing, vagrancy laws were repressive.[23]

Henry's reformation was not smooth, and the years from 1534 to 1647, when George Fox began his ministry, had many ups and downs. Henry promoted a reformed church that was hardly distinguishable from the Roman Catholic tradition. Edward VI attempted to complete the religious revolution,[24] making the church much more Protestant. At the death of Edward, the next monarch, Mary Tudor (Bloody Mary),[25] did her best to restore Catholicism. However, Elizabeth I, who reigned as queen from 1558 to 1603, created a compromise called the Elizabethan Settlement. Yet much that she gained was lost when, because she had no heir, the throne went to the Stuarts of Scotland: James I and Charles I. In 1642, a civil war began that saw the execution of King Charles I. With the end of the monarchy came a commonwealth government,

[22] James I, when he inherited the realm of England, was uncertain whether the Church of England was Catholic or Reformed. See, Diarmaid MacCulloch. *Christianity: The First Three Thousand Years* (New York: Viking, 2009), 647

[23] Arthur Lyon Cross, *A Shorter History of England and Great Britain* (New York: MacMillan Company, 1939), 231-232.

[24] Cross, 230.

[25] Mary, the oldest daughter of Henry VIII and Catharine of Aragon, reigned from 1553 to 1558 as Mary I of England. She was intent on reversing the reformation begun by her father. The title "Bloody Mary" was applied because of the number of Protestants and other religious dissenters that she burned at the stake. See Carolly Erickson, *Bloody Mary; the Life of Mary Tudor* (New York: William Morrow, 1978).

the dismissal of four parliaments, and considerable conflict and confusion.

During the time of Edward VI and his attempts to increase the Reformation, many foreigners flooded into England—"Lutherans from Germany, Calvinists from Geneva, Zwinglians from Zurich, as well as 'heretics of every hue,'"—which added to the turmoil and confusion.[26] When Mary became queen in 1553, and attempted to turn England back to Roman Catholicism, she gave all of them just twenty-four days to leave the country. Most of them did so, settling into the centers of Calvinism on the continent and then returning to England when Elizabeth ascended the throne (thus, bringing back with them stronger Calvinistic convictions).[27]

Elizabeth is said to have had, "no sympathy with the advanced Protestantism of Edward's reign and still less with Mary's Roman Catholic restoration."[28] Religion meant little to her, but moderation and united effort meant everything. Her great achievement is known as the Elizabethan Settlement. It was a religious and political compromise that established the Church of England. Elizabeth realized that to follow the Protestant extremes of Edward VI or the Catholic extremes of Mary would only continue to bring turmoil and disunity.[29] Thus, she found a middle way that kept the Church of England a Protestant church but retained many Catholic

---

[26] Cross, *Shorter History*, 231.

[27] Ibid., 240. Those who fled the country were known as the Marian exiles. See also Qualben, 325-326.

[28] Cross, 243.

[29] Walter Phelps Hall, Robert Greenhalgh Abion and Jennie Barnes Pope, *A History of England and the Empire-Commonwealth* (Boston: Blaisdell Publishing, 1961), 196

practices.[30] Elizabeth was queen from 1558 to 1603; forty-five years of relative peace.[31]

Because Elizabeth died without an heir, the crown went to James VI of Scotland, who became James I of England. James had a much stronger approach to the religious situation than Elizabeth. Shortly after becoming king, he gathered all the religious leaders together at a conference at Hampton Court (1604) and was successful at pacifying the reformers and "cracking the whip" on the bishops. He was on record as "a master prepared to interest himself in the minutia of church discipline, worship and administration, and to approach matters of religion with a more open mind than Elizabeth."[32] His one great achievement was the publication of what became known as the King James Version of the Bible.[33]

His son, Charles I, who took the throne in 1625, was less judicious than his father in his approach to church administration and allowed his close friend, William Laud (promoted by Charles to the Archbishop of Canterbury), a free hand as most historians suggest "with disastrous results."[34] Laud firmly believed any opposition came from a "Puritan Conspiracy" and his high-handed tactics so angered the people that many fled the country to set up colonies

---

[30] Latourette, 810.

[31] Hall, 197.

[32] J. P. Kenyon, *The Pelican History of England; Stuart England*, 2nd ed., (New York: Penguin Books, 1988), 59. While Kenyon suggests that the Hampton Court Conference was a successful one for James, Walter Hall (*A History of England and the Empire-Commonwealth*) declared that no good came from the conference except for the idea of the King James translation. See also Latourette, 816-817 or Cross, 288.

[33] Hall, 215. See also MacCulloch, 650.

[34] MacCulloch, 650; Latourette, 819.

in the Americas (hence, "New England"). The religious question was exacerbated by Charles' marriage to Henrietta Maria of Spain, a devoted Catholic, who had a tremendous influence on the king and a direct involvement in increasing Catholicism.[35]

The obstinacy and political blundering of King Charles I and his open conflict with the Puritans (a reforming body within the Church of England), eventually led to a civil war (1642-1646) that resulted in execution of Charles I and the establishment of a religious commonwealth led by Oliver Cromwell.

The Puritans comprised a reform effort that arose in the time of Queen Elizabeth. They were not satisfied with the Elizabethan Settlement, and longed for a purer form of worship, a different form of church government, and a revision of the standard doctrine. The goal was to transform the Church of England into a Calvinistic body.[36] These "Puritans" became quite active in the reign of James I, often protesting the king's encouragement of sports on Sundays and the form of worship the king promoted. These clashes became major controversies with Charles I. It was the Puritans who formed the commonwealth government that ruled England after the execution of Charles I until the restoration with Charles II in 1660.

Into this milieu, the Lord raised up one to publish the truth. In the year 1635, young George Fox became eleven years old. Fox recorded in his autobiography that "when I came to eleven years of age I knew pureness and righteousness; for while a child I was taught how to walk to be kept pure. The Lord taught me to be faithful in all things, and to act faithfully two ways, viz. inwardly, to

---

[35] Hall, 224.

[36] Qualben, 326.

God, and outwardly, to man; and to keep to Yea and Nay in all things."[37] God was preparing the hero, the leader, to gather his people. In 1647, when George Fox was twenty-three years old, he began that gathering.

---

[37] George Fox, *Journal of George Fox,* ed. Rufus Jones (Richmond: Friends United Press, 1976), 66.

Discussion Questions/Projects

1. What thoughts do you have about your being a part of the long, historic tradition of Christ's church?

2. A number of religious groups are mentioned in the chapter—Baptists, Fifth Monarchists, Levellers, Puritans, Ranters, Quakers, Seekers, Separatists. What were the goals and successes of each of these?

3. After research can you fill in additional details for each of the historical periods given for Church History? What personalities, events, issues, or great ideas characterize each period?

4. Only a small proportion of the reform efforts that happened before the Reformation of 1517 are mentioned. With research can you make a more complete list?

5. The Reformation in England differed considerably from the reforms carried out in Germany, and elsewhere. Why and in what ways?

6. Puritanism is difficult to define. Some see it as any who opposed the Church of England. Some see it as a movement to purify the Church of England. Others focus on the strict observance of church regulations that affected day to day life. What do you understand the term "Puritan" to mean?

7. We do not know the political, religious, and social turmoil that Fox experienced, but how do you imagine you might have felt as a child, growing up in such an environment?

For Further Study

Bacon, Margaret. *The Quiet Rebels: The Story of the Quakers in America.* New York: Basic Books, 1969.

Cairns, Earle E. *Christianity Through the Centuries.* Grand Rapids: Zondervan, 1996.

Chambers, Mortimer, Raymond Grew, David Herlihy, Theodore Rabb and Isser Woloch. *The Western Experience*. 4th Ed. New York: Knopf, 1987.

Cross, Arthur Lyon. *A Shorter History of England and Great Britain*. New York: MacMillan Company, 1939.

Fox, George. *Journal of George Fox*. Edited by Rufus Jones. Richmond: Friends United Press, 1976.

Hall, Walter Phelps, Robert Greenhalgh Abion and Jennie Barnes Pope. *A History of England and the Empire-Commonwealth*. Boston: Blaisdell Publishing, 1961.

Jones, Rufus. *George Fox: Seeker and Friend*. New York: Harper, 1930.

Kenyon, J. P. *The Pelican History of England: Stuart England*. 2nd Ed. New York: Penguin Books, 1988.

Latourette, Kenneth Scott. *A History of Christianity*. New York: Harper & Row, 1953.

McNair, Philip. "Seeds of Renewal." In the *Introduction to Christianity*, edited by Tom Dowley. New York: Fortress Press, 2002.

Qualben, Lars. *A History of the Christian Church*. New York: Thomas Nelson, 1958.

Shaw, Ian J. *Christianity: The Biography: 2,000 years of Global History*. Grand Rapids: Zondervan, 2016.

Stevenson, William. *The Story of the Reformation*. Lousiville: John Knox Press, 1959.

Vos, Howard F. *Exploring Church History*. Nashville: Thomas Nelson, 1994.

_____. *Highlights of Church History*. Chicago: Moody Press, 1960.

Robert Withers (Widders) 1618 (?) - 1686

Reading through the *Journal of George Fox*, one comes regularly upon the name, Robert Withers (also spelled Widders). He was one of the first to join George Fox and became one of the most vigorous of the Friends preachers. George often stopped by his home not far from Lancaster and Robert from the beginning was the companion of Fox on his travels. In 1671, Withers accompanied Fox and ten others on the two-year trip to Barbados, Jamaica, and several of the American colonies. The events of that trip were daily dictated to Withers and one other, so that it was Withers who kept one of two diaries.[38]

Fox recorded in his *Journal*: "He was not much in declaration" (i.e. nothing of a preacher), but burly, fearless, imperturbable, and humorous, he was a much-sought companion. "His very countenance and eye was refreshment and comfort."[39] Fox called him "the Thundering man,"[40] for his staunch, downright spirit made him a pillar of strength, when facing evil-doers.

"In 1663 Robert Withers for going to a meeting at Yealand was sent to prison for nine weeks [and was] fined £3 6s. 8d. for which the bailiff took two sows worth £6 10s. Nine other Friends were charged at the same time." "Withers' sufferings from distraint and spoilings exceeded those of any other Friend, yet Thomas Camm said: "I never saw him in the least concerned and dejected when his cattle, corn and household goods were, as it were, by wholesale

---

[38] George Fox, *The Journal of George Fox,* rev. ed., John Nickalls, ed. (Cambridge: Cambridge University Press, 1952), 609.

[39] B. Nightingale, *Early Stages of the Quaker Movement in Lancaster*, retrieved from https://archive.org/.

[40] George Fox, *The Autobiography of George Fox from His Journal*, Henry Stanley Newman, ed. (London: S. W. Partridge and Company, 1886), 155.

swept away." [41]

"I have known him 34 years," wrote Margaret Fell at his death, "He was a dear and faithful brother to me and my children in all our trials and sufferings. He would not have failed to come and see us, night or day, over two dangerous sands, if it had been in the deep of winter; many a time hath he done so of his own accord; and for the most part I have been sensible of his coming before he came, so near and dear was he unto me." [42]

"His was a large nobility mixed with a lamblike innocency which was as a garment of praise upon him and made him right lovely in the eyes of the upright," wrote Thomas Camm.[43] After Withers' death, his own meeting, together with George Fox and his wife, published a short testimony to him. Sixteen men and women of Yealand meeting wrote simple tributes.[44] "I have been prisoner with him several times at Lancaster," wrote Thomas Beakbayne, "and his cheerful countenance and good example and advice to Friends always administered strength and comfort."[45]

---

[41] Elizabeth Brockbank, "The Story of Quakerism in the Lancaster District," *The Journal of the Friend's Historical Society*, Volume XXXVI, p. 12.

[42] Ibid., 9.

[43] Ibid., 12.

[44] Ibid., 10.

[45] Ibid.

2
George Fox

> 1624 born at Fenny Drayton in Leicestershire, England
> 1643 Fox leaves home to become a stranger to all.
> 1646 realizes the need to know Christ
> 1647 begins ministry in Mansfield and Nottinghamshire
> 1650 the first imprisonment
> 1652 the Pendle Hill vision
> 1655 meets with Oliver Cromwell
> 1657 preaches in Wales and Scotland
> 1662 The Conventicle Act imprisons many Friends.
> 1671 Fox leaves for North America.
> 1677 visits Holland and Germany
> 1691 dies in London

In 1624, just a year before King Charles I ascended the throne, George Fox was born at Drayton-in-the-Clay,[46] Leicestershire, England, to humble and sincere parents, Christopher and Mary Fox. His father Christopher was known among the neighbors as "Righteous Christer,"[47] and George acknowledges in his *Journal*, "There was the seed of God in him."[48] His mother appears to have

---

[46]Drayton-in-the-Clay is now known as Fenny Drayton and is still a small village in the Midlands of England.

[47] Fox, *Autobiography*, 1. See also, George Fox, *The Journal of George* Fox, Rufus Jones, ed. (Richmond: Friends United Press, 1976), 65.

[48] George Fox, *Journal,* retrieved from
https://archive.org/stream/journalofgeorgef00foxg/journalofgeorgef00foxg_dj
vu.txt

been a very devout person.[49] Young George emulated the spiritual example his parents gave him becoming a spiritually sensitive young man, faithful both inwardly to God and outwardly to others.[50]

George recognized the work of the Lord within him from an early age. The prologue to his *Journal* indicates this: "I think fit," he wrote, "before I proceed to set forth my public travels in the service of the truth, briefly to mention how it was with me in my youth, and how the work of the Lord was begun, and gradually carried on in me, even from my childhood."[51] William Penn wrote of him: "From a child he appeared of another frame of mind than the rest of his brethren; being more religious, inward, still, solid, and observing, beyond his years . . . especially in divine things."[52]

The work of the Lord had begun early in him, and, as a teenager, he began to question the validity of the religion he encountered around him. He saw the grave faces of the elderly men worshipping in the village church, yet then saw them during the week as they tumbled out of the ale-house, and he wondered at their religion. He saw others sharing in worship but dealing unjustly in the marketplace, and some who made gluttons of themselves while others starved. Again, he wondered "how can this be?" What was

---

[49] William Penn in the introduction to the *Journal* describes George's parents as "honest and sufficient" and indicates the Christian nurture of both, especially George's mother, Mary.

[50] *Journal of George Fox,* Rufus Jones, 66.

[51] Fox, *Autobiography,* 1.

[52] William Penn, "The Testimony of William Penn Concerning That Faithful Servant George Fox," as preface to *The Journal of George Fox,* Rufus Jones, ed., (Richmond: Friends United Press, 1976). See also: https://www.christianitytoday.com/history/people/denominationalfounders/george-fox.html

religion to mean?[53]

As a young man, Fox endeavored to keep his words few and seasoned with grace, not to eat and to drink to make himself wanton but for health, to wrong no one, and to always make his "yea" yea and his "nay" nay. He used the word "verily" in all his dealings and "it was a common saying among people who knew him: "If George says, 'verily,' there is no altering him.""[54]

Grieved at the actions of a cousin and a friend who entrapped him in a drinking bout George, unable to sleep, "walked . . . and prayed, and cried to the Lord" and the Lord said to him, "forsake all young and old, keep out of all, and be as a stranger unto all."[55] And, he did. At nineteen years of age, in 1643 (the second year of the English Civil War),[56] he left home in an effort to find himself and the answers for the many questions he had. He became a seeker.

After returning home without having found his answers, friends and family had their answers for him. He would settle his grieving soul, they said, by getting married, chewing tobacco, or joining the army. Solitary walks and hours spent with an open Bible gave him insights and a mastery of the written word, and in 1647 he found his answer. Here is his testimony:

---

[53] Elfrida Vipont. *The Story of Quakerism, 1652-1952*. (Richmond: Friends United Press, 1977), 17-19.

[54] Fox, *Autobiography*, 1; *Journal*, 67.

[55] Fox, *Autobiography*, 2; *Journal*, 68.

[56] Charles I so angered Parliament and the people that Civil War began in 1642. In 1644 and 1645 much of the war happened in the area where George Fox was. See John Punshon, *Portrait in Grey: A Short History of the* Quakers, 2nd ed., (Fitchburg: Quaker Books, 2006), 37.

But as I had forsaken the priests, so I also left the separate preachers, and those called the most experienced people; for I saw there was none among them all that could speak to my condition. And when all my hopes in them and in all men were gone, so that I had nothing outwardly to help me, nor could tell what to do, then, oh then, I heard a voice which said, "There is one, even Christ Jesus, that can speak to thy condition." When I heard it, my heart did leap for joy.[57]

Filled with joy Fox also was given understanding:

Then the Lord let me see why there was none upon the earth that could speak to my condition, namely, that I might give Him all the glory. For all are concluded under sin, and shut up in unbelief, as I had been, that Jesus Christ might have the pre-eminence, who enlightens, and gives grace, faith, and power. Thus, when God doth work, who shall hinder? This I knew experimentally. My desires after the Lord grew stronger, and zeal in the pure knowledge of God, and of Christ alone, without the help of any man, book, or writing.[58]

His three years of searching brought him to a great "opening"[59] that would send him on mission for the rest of his life. He now knew that Christ was not a dead Christ, but a living one, and that Christ's

---

[57] Fox, *Autobiography*, 6-7; *Journal*, 82.

[58] Fox, *Autobiography*, 6-7; *Journal*, 82.

[59] The term "opening" as George Fox used it means a flash of insight or a clear understanding of a truth.

work for humankind's salvation had not ended on the cross. Christ was present in the world and would teach and lead his people. Fox's role was to direct people to Christ by "declaring truth" among them.[60]

Fox began to declare truth immediately, beginning his ministry in Mansfield and Nottinghamshire. His *Journal* records his first public declaration at Duckenfield: "I declared truth among them. There were some convinced, who received the Lord's teaching, by which they were confirmed and stood in the truth." Then he moved on to attend a large gathering of Baptists at Broughton in Leicestershire of which he said: "The Lord opened my mouth and His everlasting truth was declared amongst them, and the power of the Lord was over them all."[61]In the *Journal* Fox many times noted that there were those who were convinced, and he repeatedly credited this to the fact that the "power of the Lord was overall." "The Lord's power broke forth," is another expression Fox used of his early ministry, "and I spoke to them of the things of God, which they heard with attention and silence and went away and spread the fame thereof."[62]

From his 1647 "opening," George Fox moved around Northern England as an itinerant preacher, exhorting seekers to listen to the voice of Christ.[63] His ministry was characterized by speaking in

---

[60] See Rufus Jones, *George Fox: Seeker and Friend*, (New York: Harper and Brothers Publishers, 1930), 21. Declaring truth is an expression used often in the *Journal*.

[61] Fox, *Autobiography*, 8; *Journal*, 85-86.

[62] Fox, *Autobiography*, p. 9.

[63] Arthur Roberts, "George Fox and the Quaker (Friends) Movement," retrieved from https://www.georgefox.edu/about/history/quakers.html

churches (which Fox called "steeple-houses") at the end of the sermon, addressing large groups of men and women in outdoor meetings, and speaking directly to small groups and individuals. In his words: "Thus I travelled in the Lord's service, as He led me."[64]

He followed the Lord's leading and went wherever he was moved. For example, consider this excerpt from his *Journal*:

> Moreover, I was moved to go to several courts and steeple-houses at Mansfield and other places, to warn them to leave off oppression and oaths, and to turn from deceit to the Lord, and do justly. Particularly at Mansfield, after I had been at a court there, I was moved to go and speak to one of the wickedest men in the country, one who was a common drunkard; and I reproved him, in the dread of the mighty God, for his evil courses. When I had done speaking, and left him, he came after me, and told me he was so smitten when I spoke to him that he had scarce any strength left in him. So this man was convinced, turned from his wickedness, and remained an honest, sober man, to the astonishment of the people who had known him before. Thus the work of the Lord went forward, and many were turned from darkness to light . . . Divers meetings of Friends, in several places, were then gathered to God's teaching, by His light, Spirit, and power: for the Lord's power broke forth daily more and more wonderfully.[65]

---

[64] Fox, *Autobiography*, 14.

[65] Fox, *Autobiography*, 12; *Journal*, 96.

This itinerant ministry resulted in many people being convinced, but also in many abuses suffered by Fox at the hands of the Anglican church, as well as other independent sects who opposed his message. He was thrown down church steps, beaten with sticks, and once was struck in the face with a brass-bound Bible. He spent six months in Derby jail, he was "offered release if he would accept a commission in Cromwell's army, Fox refused, saying Christ had brought him into the 'covenant of peace.' For this he was jailed another six months."[66]

In 1652, in the fourth year of Oliver Cromwell's commonwealth, George Fox received a vision from the Lord after he had climbed Pendle Hill (an outcropping of rock in Northern England).[67] From that height, the Lord showed him "a people in white raiment coming to the Lord." Since Fox had begun his ministry a number of small groups of believers had been formed. Calling themselves "Children of Light" and "Friends of Truth," these became the nucleus of the Society of Friends which Fox gave leadership to. In 1652, these small groups began to merge and indeed a great people began to be gathered to the Lord.

In the months before June 1652, George Fox had been extremely busy, going dale to dale and speaking to anyone he found. He was "largely and freely" declaring "the word of life unto them" with not much persecution. He passed through the dales, "warning people to fear God." On June 13th, he attended a First day gathering at Firbank Chapel in Westmoreland. He did not enter the chapel, but

---

[66] Roberts, "George Fox."

[67] Pendle Hill is a moorland ridge on the border between Lancashire and Yorkshire in Northern England. The summit is at 1830 feet. Walter Williams, *The Rich Heritage of Quakerism* (Newberg: Barclay Press, 1987), 1.

after the morning meeting, he used a rock near the chapel as a pulpit and "declared God's everlasting truth and word of life freely and largely for about the space of three hours" to all those who gathered around him. It was judged that there were a thousand people present that day who listened to Fox as he "directed all to the Spirit of God in themselves."[68] This meeting at Firbank Fell is considered by many to be the actual beginning of the Quaker movement.[69] Fox recorded after the meeting: "Very largely was I opened at this meeting; the Lord's convincing power accompanied my ministry, and reached home to the hearts of the people; whereby many were convinced, and all the teachers of that congregation (who were many) were convinced of God's everlasting truth."[70]

From 1652 until 1671, George Fox made several circuits around England declaring the truth of the Lord, encouraging Friends, and more than once spending a length of time in jail or prison. In 1656 and 1657, he took the gospel to Wales and Scotland. In 1658 and 1659, he ministered in London. From 1660, with the restoration of Charles II, Fox made several circuits that covered Northern England, and the middle and southern portions of the country. A good portion of this time, when he himself was not in jail, he was writing letters to the king and others on behalf of the many other Friends

---

[68] Fox, *Autobiography*, 46-49; *Journal*, 151-155.

[69] Peter Blood, "Firbank Fell's Challenge to 21st-Century Quakerism," retrieved from http://www.inwardlight.org/firbank_fell_challenge.html. Peter writes: "On Sunday, June 13th, 1652, about a thousand people gathered on an isolated hillside in rural northern England to listen to a little-known but charismatic young man named George Fox preach. The sermon lasted three hours. It is always risky to look for a particular date on which a religious movement is born, but many choose this as the time Quakerism was born."

[70] Fox, *Autobiography*, 48.

who were imprisoned. From 1671 to 1673, he visited Friends and openly declared the truth to hundreds in Barbados, Jamaica, and most of the colonies in America.

Mansfield, Nottingham, Derby, Carlisle, Doomsdale (Launceston Castle), Lancaster, Leicester, Scarborough, and Worcester: these are the jails or prisons that Fox found himself in for a good number of months.[71] He was imprisoned because he interrupted a church service. He was accused of blasphemy because he spoke of Christ in him. He was jailed for breaking social norms, such as refusing to show deference by removing his hat or addressing a person of importance with a plural "you." Mostly, he was imprisoned because he would not take an oath. The charges were numerous. The Blasphemy Act, passed in 1650, forbade any testimony that would claim a special relationship with God (as "Christ in me") or that would deny the authority of Scripture and Fox and the Friends declared the Spirit over the Scriptures. The Oath of Supremacy required one to swear allegiance and Friends understood Christ said, "swear not at all." The Conventicle Act of 1664 forbade any religious gathering of more than five people. Friends, therefore, were not able to gather legally. Thus, on more than one occasion George Fox would be apprehended while preaching, hauled before the authorities, and then made to wait in jail for the court sessions to be held. Often told that there were warrants out for his arrest, he would enter a city nevertheless, in obedience to the Lord and the call to publish truth.

George Fox had an indomitable spirit which, once it had received its call, shied away from nothing. The call to declare truth was constantly obeyed. Fox never slacked off nor backed down. Marshalls,

---

[71] For a detailed list of imprisonments, see Jones, *Seeker and Friend*, 96.

justices, soldiers, priests, and angry professors—he encountered all of them with boldness and yet also with kindness and no rancor. According to Rufus Jones: "He never toned down his proclamation to make it more palatable." Jones adds: "He positively challenged almost every entrenched form and established practice of his time."[72] The guards at Scarborough Castle said of him: "He is stiff as a tree and as pure as a bell; for we never could bow him."[73] His spirit was sensitive: sensitive to the whispering of the Holy Spirit, sensitive to the needs of Friends, and of people—whoever and wherever. H. L. Mackay said of him: "George Fox never lost his temper—he left that to his opponents."[74]

Coupled with this spirit was an amazing stamina, for he spoke to crowds almost daily. He covered nearly the whole of England in his travel, including both Scotland and Wales in his itinerary. Though travel was strenuous, he covered a good part of the American colonies on his two-year visit there. Even when his health was lagging, as a result of the harsh conditions experienced in his imprisonments, he pushed on.

Without question, he was honest and trustworthy. When Justice Bennett and the jailer at Derby, both of whom felt he need not be incarcerated, granted him walking privileges, they may have hoped that he would take advantage and use the opportunity to escape. However, they discovered he was not that kind of prisoner.[75] If he said he would get himself to the court he would (and did).

---

[72] Ibid., 90.

[73] Quoted in L. V. Hodgkin, *A Book of Quaker Saints*, (London: Longman, 1968), 33. The quote is found in the *Journal*.

[74] Ibid., 24.

[75] Vipont, 23.

His knowledge of the Bible was extraordinary and bewildering to his opponents,[76] and he often used the Scriptures to quiet his critics. Gerard Croese, a non-Quaker Dutch historian, has said: "Though the Bible were lost, it might be found in the mouth of George Fox."[77] The discourses he sent to Friends and his writings left on record behind him were mostly texts of Scripture. We find his testimony in the *Journal*: "But I brought them Scriptures, and told them there was an anointing within man to teach him, and that the Lord would teach His people Himself."[78] T. Canby Jones states: "The Bible which Fox practically memorized and quoted most often was the "new" or "modern" translation of his day, the *King James Version* of 1611 . . . In the tracts which he wrote at that time Fox often quotes the King James version from memory. "[79]

---

[76] Alfred Brayshaw, *The Personality of George Fox* (London: Allenson & Co., 1933).

[77] T. Canby Jones, "The Bible. Its Authority and Dynamic in George Fox and Contemporary Quakerism," *Quaker Religious Thought*, 7 (1): 18-36. Retrieved from https://digitalcommons.georgefox.edu.

[78] Fox, *Autobiography*, 5: ("shewed them by the scriptures"); *Journal*, 76.

[79] T. Canby Jones, *Personality of George Fox*.

Discussion Questions/Projects

1. George Fox travelled many miles by foot seeking spiritual counsel and was discouraged that much advice was not helpful. How do you determine if the spiritual counsel others give you is good and according to God's will?

2. Old men behaving lightly and wantonly toward each other; people solemn and worshipful on Sunday but tipsy and boisterous in the week; people holy on Sunday but cheating in the marketplace; Elfrida Vipont gives these examples of inconsistencies that troubled George Fox. What are the parallels for this century? Are they the same? Do they cause you the same discomfort they did George Fox?

3. George Fox was born just a year before Charles I became king. He sought the Lord in the midst of a Civil War. He began his ministry almost at the same time the king was executed and during his time the government became a commonwealth and then was restored back to a monarchy. How did these political changes affect George Fox and his ability to minister?

4. Fox said about his transforming experience: "There is one, even Christ Jesus that can speak to thy condition." What does this statement mean to you? Can you say the same about yourself?

5. Describe George Fox's understanding of the Scriptures in relationship to the Holy Spirit. Fox was imprisoned the first time because he interrupted a preacher in a steeple-house who had an understanding different than that of Fox. What did the preacher believe was the role of Scripture? See Fox's *Journal* for the early ministry at Mansfield.

6. The great three-hour meeting at Firbank Fell is in a very real sense the beginning of the great movement that began the gathering those Fox had seen from Pendle Hill into the Kingdom of God. In Fox's *Journal* account he used several expressions that can be used to describe his life's ministry. Examine the account in the *Journal* just previous to that of Firbank Fell and the account of

Firbank Fell from an unabridged copy of the *Journal* making a list of these expressions. (See footnote #42 below for a website for an online copy.) *Autobiography*, pp. 46-48, *Journal*, pp. 154-156.

7. Do you have deep-seated beliefs that you would be willing to remain in prison under terrible conditions and not make a compromise for? Was it right for Fox to refuse to swear allegiance? What is our stand on oaths and swearing in the 21st century?

8. In 1671 George Fox made a two-year journey to the Americas and visited Friends meetings in Barbados, Jamaica, and in a number of the American colonies. Which of the American colonies at that time had Friends Meetings? What Friends were responsible for planting these meetings? You may want to refer to Chapter 18 in the *Journal* edited by Rufus Jones or Chapter 27 in the *Autobiography* edited by Newman.

9. A number of character traits are used in this chapter to describe George Fox. Compose a list of these and give an example from his *Journal*, if possible, for each. What other traits can you list for him? Using your list can you compose a closing paragraph for this chapter?

10. George Fox did not marry until 1669 when he was forty-five. He married Judge Fell's widow, Margaret Fell, the mother of nine children. Discover what you can of this marriage. How long were they together until duty set them apart? Where was George while Margaret was in prison? In what ways did George support the ministry of Margaret?

For Further Study

Barbour, Hugh and J. William Frost. *The Quakers.* Richmond: Friends United Press, 1994.

Fox, George. *The Autobiography of George Fox from His Journal.* Edited by Henry Stanley Newman. London: S. W. Partridge

2

3

and Company, 1886.

_____. *The Journal of George Fox.* Edited by Rufus Jones. Richmond: Friends United Press, 1976.

Hodgkin, L. V. *A Book of Quaker Saints.* London: Longmans, 1968.

Jones, Rufus. *George Fox: Seeker and Friend.* New York: Harper and Brothers, 1930.

Punshon, John. *Portrait in Grey: A Short History of the Quakers.* 2nd ed. Fitchburg: Quaker Books, 2006.

Roberts, Arthur. *Through Flaming Sword: A Spiritual Biography of George Fox.* Newberg: Barclay Press, 2008.

Vipont, Elfrida. *The Story of Quakerism, 1652-1952.* Richmond: Friends United Press, 1977.

Williams, Walter R. *The Rich Heritage of Quakerism.* Newberg: Barclay Press, 1987.

Edward Burrough 1634-1663

The name Edward Burrough[80] is found numerous times in Fox's Journal as one who was with George Fox. He was an early English Quaker leader and controversialist. He is regarded as one of the Valiant Sixty, early Quaker preachers and missionaries.

Burrough was born in Underbarrow, Cumbria, and educated in the Church of England, but became a Presbyterian before converting to Quakerism. He heard George Fox preach in 1652 and immediately converted during his late teens. He was consequently rejected by his parents. Burrough began itinerant preaching throughout England, traveling with another Friend, Francis Howgill.

During the years 1656-1657, Burrough and John Bunyan were engaged in a debate by way of pamphlets. First Bunyan published *Some Gospel Truths Opened* in which he attacked Quaker beliefs. Burrough responded with *The True Faith of the Gospel of Peace*. Bunyan countered Burrough's pamphlet with *A Vindication of Some Gospel Truths Opened*, which Burrough answered with *Truth (the Strongest of All) Witnessed Forth*.[81] Later the Quaker leader George Fox entered the verbal fray by publishing a refutation of Bunyan's essay in his *The Great Mystery of the Great Whore Unfolded*.

Upon the Restoration, in 1660, Burrough approached King Charles II to find protection and relief of Quakers in New England, who were then being persecuted by the Puritans. Charles granted him an audience in 1661, and was persuaded to issue a writ stopping

---

[80] Burrough is sometimes found spelled Burroughs.

[81] Edward Burrough wrote several books. One, *The Memoir of the Life and Religious Labors of Edward Burrough,* is a religious classic. This book is available online at: www.hallvworthington.com/Burrough/Memoir1.html

(temporarily) the corporal and capital punishments of the Quakers in Massachusetts. Burrough arranged for the writ to be delivered by Samuel Shattuck, himself a Quaker under ban from Massachusetts. Charles' writ commanded the Massachusetts authorities to send the imprisoned Quakers to England for trial, but they chose instead to release them. The king's order effectively stopped the hangings, but imprisonments and floggings were resumed the next year.

In 1662, Burrough was arrested for holding a meeting, which was illegal under the terms of the Conventicle Act.[82] He was sent to Newgate Prison, London. An order for his release signed by Charles II was ignored by the local authorities, and Burrough remained in Newgate until his death on February 14, 1663, aged just 29.

---

[82] The Oath of Allegiance Act of 1662 (which required Quakers to swear an oath of allegiance to the king.)

Elizabeth Hooton 1600-1673

George Fox records, as he went through Derbyshire in 1647, that he met with a tender people, and a very tender woman whose name was Elizabeth Hooton.[83] Elizabeth Hooton was a member of a Baptist group when she met George Fox. Attracted by the message of Fox, she began to hold meetings in her home so that the other Baptists could hear the same message. These who met with her became known as the "Children of Light." She became one of the first preachers of the Valiant Sixty and the first woman preacher of the Quakers.[84]

Elizabeth was imprisoned in Derby in 1651 for "reproving a priest." In 1652, she was jailed for sixteen months in York for preaching in the church at Rotherham. In 1654, she was put in prison in Lincolnshire for speaking to priest Joseph Thurston; six months for speaking to him in the steeple-house and, later, twelve weeks for speaking to him after the morning exercise.[85]

She was literate and wrote letters to judges and other public officials. When in jail in Lincoln Castle in 1654, she wrote a letter to the authorities there protesting conditions in the prison and calling for separation of the sexes and useful employment for the

---

[83] George Fox, *The Journal of George Fox,* rev. ed., John Nickalls, ed.

(Cambridge: Cambridge University Press, 1952)

[84] "Elizabeth Hooton: 1600-1672," Quakers in the World,

http://www.quakersintheworld.org/quakers-in-action/223/Elizabeth-Hooton.

[85] Emily Manners, *Elizabeth Hooton: First Quaker Woman Preacher (1600-1672)* (London: Headley Bros., 1914). Retrieved from

https://archive.org/stream/elizabethhootonf00mann#page/n5/mode/2up.

prisoners.[86]

In 1661, at the age of sixty, Elizabeth went to New England and urged better treatment of Quakers there. With another woman she attempted to visit Quaker prisoners when she and her companion were themselves imprisoned for days without food, put in the stocks and beaten in three towns, then taken into the wilderness and left. The two women survived by following wolf tracks through the snow till they found a settlement.[87]

Back in England, Hooton followed the king to his tennis court and there petitioned him to redress the suffering Quakers in New England. She must have won the King's respect, because he gave her a document authorizing her to buy land in Massachusetts and use it to make a safe haven for Quakers in the colony.[88] The authorities in Massachusetts did not allow this.

In 1672, Elizabeth was with George Fox in Jamaica. Fox fell ill on the voyage and Hooton acted as his nurse. However, within one week of their arrival, in Jamaica, she herself fell suddenly ill and died the next day. Fox wrote of her death: "Elizabeth Hooton, a woman of great age, who had travelled much in Truth's service, and suffered much for it, departed this life. She was well the day before she died, and departed in peace, like a lamb, bearing testimony to Truth at her departure."[89]

---

[86] Ibid., 6-7, 14.

[87] Hooton, Quakers in the World.

[88] Ibid.

[89] Fox, *Autobiography*, 243.

3
16th-Century Anabaptists; 17th-Century Quakers[90]

1517 The Reformation begins with Martin Luther.

1518 Zwingli begins the Reformation in Switzerland.

1525 The Anabaptists are re-baptized to show their conviction that baptism required of adults not infants.

1534 Excesses happen at Münster.

1536 Menno Simmons joins the Anabaptist and later leads the Mennonites.

1647 George Fox begins ministry in Mansfield and Nottinghamshire.

1652 George Fox has vision at Pendle Hill.

1652 In June at Firbank Fell many begin to be added to the Quaker movement.

In the sixteenth century, "Anabaptist" came to be synonymous with distortion of truth, opposition to God, and danger to the established order.[91] In the seventeenth century, the word used was "Quaker."

How did this come to be? That both the Anabaptist movement of the sixteenth century and the Quaker movement, a century later,

---

[90] This chapter was originally written by the author on 7-30-1986 for a seminar.

[91] Harold J. Grimm, *The Reformation Era, 1500-1650* (New York: Macmillan, 1973), 268.

came to bear opprobrious names and reputations might be because of their very similar purpose, role, and consequence in history. Both have left a very definite impact. The people and the results of each differ significantly from the reputation they had with their contemporaries.

The term "Anabaptist" means one who re-baptizes or baptizes again (*ana* being Greek for again) and was an insulting name given to a group of believers who felt that infant baptism as practiced by the Catholic Church and continued in the Lutheran and Zwinglian Reformations was both useless and unscriptural. How can infants know anything of salvation? Cannot baptism only have meaning as a sign of repentance and a transformed life to someone who can understand? Are not adults, not infants, to be baptized?

A small group of believers in Switzerland began to think this way during the beginnings of the reformation in Zurich; they became known as the Swiss Brethren. Conversing with Zwingli they could not convince him of their position and the issue then came to public debate. Unfortunately, they were judged to be the ones who lost and were ordered to conform, leave Zurich, or face imprisonment.[92]

On January 21, 1525, a small group (there may have been as many as twenty four) of these brethren including Conrad Grebel, Feliz Mantz, George Blaurock (Cajacob), and Micheal Sattler, met in Felix Mantz's home to consider the ultimatum and decided to

---

[92] Cornelius J. Dyck, *An Introduction to Mennonite History: A Popular History of the Anabaptists and the Mennonites.* (Scottdale: Herald Press, 1981), 49.

answer it with action—they would all prove their convictions for adult baptism by being baptized. This is what they did. Conrad Grebel baptized George Blaurock and George, in turn, baptized each of the others.

This defiant act put them against the authorities and the inevitable persecution took place, but not until after their action had attracted many others and a movement was begun. It was not so much a movement to insist upon adult baptism, however, as it was an attempt to restore primitive Christianity. They were concerned with Christian life; a life patterned after the teachings and example of Christ, a life they did not see in the Reformation, even though it emphasized faith. One has said: "it seems certain that the fundamental aim of all the brethren was a return to the pattern of early Christianity."[93]

Baptism was only one of the concerns they held. They were interested in making practical applications of biblical teachings to all of the affairs of this world,[94] and as they gathered in small determined groups—determined to live out their convictions— they were persecuted, some killed, others imprisoned, and many forced to flee. But their concepts and teachings grew. Others were persuaded to join them. Persecution helped them grow and as they spread they divided into a number of distinct groups.

There were the Swiss Brethren, who first started in Switzerland and spread into Austria and Germany. There were the Hutterites,

---

[93] William Stevenson, *The Story of the* Reformation (Louisville: John Knox Press, 1959), 63.

[94] Grimm, *Reformation,* 267.

who settled into Moravia. There were the Melchiorites, notorious for their apocalyptic kingdom in Münster in 1534-35. There were the Mennonites, primarily in the Netherlands, who under the leadership of Menno Simons tried to live down the reputation caused by the excesses at Münster.

It was easy, since they were a radical religious group, for those who stood in opposition to them to consider any new idea, any religious fanaticism, any hitherto unheard-of excess as coming from them whether it was so or not. True, there were excesses, including the interruption of church services and messages preached against whole cities (complete with object lessons, such as the preacher walking naked through the town to indicate the need for stripping away all pretensions). Often, their zeal moved ahead of their understanding, but, on the whole, they were upright, industrious, and gentle people concerned with "walking with Christ."

Although it is hard to form a compact description of their beliefs, because of the variations caused by differing locations and leaders, there are some generally agreed-upon concepts that were held by most Anabaptists.[95]

There was, first of all, the rejection of infant baptism and the use of adult baptism. This is the one tenet that gave the movement its name and that was most common to all branches. Those who met at the Mantz home, in January 1525, were the first to be re-baptized, but many others followed. Balthasar Hubmaier, a

---

[95] Williston Walker, *The Reformation* (New York: Scribner's Sons, 1900), 337-340.

reformed pastor, had his whole church re-baptized in the spring of 1525.[96] Hubmaier wrote many pamphlets in support of adult baptism; one of them being the book *On the Christian Baptism of Believers*. In early Anabaptist theology, "baptism was a covenant not only with God, but also with the congregation, whereby the members pledged to help each other in the life of obedience."[97]

The next most important belief was their definition of the church. They felt the church had to be a body of believers. The common understanding, promoted by a state-sponsored church, was that everyone within the nation was a church member, whether they believed or not. Because of their definition, Anabaptists could not support the state church, nor could they give obedience to its leadership or pay the tithe to support it. They also felt compelled to refuse to swear any oath of loyalty to the church (or to the city or state).

Thirdly, the majority believed that no Christian could bear arms and place oneself in danger of taking another's life. They believed it was the Christian's duty to suffer rather than take revenge. Thus, they could not accept positions in military or civic offices that might require them to take the sword. They also refused to be put into a position of having to judge another. They firmly held to the concept of a separated church. The church would be responsible for its own discipline, and the state, responsible for governing sinners would govern without the interference of the church.

---

[96] Dyck, *Mennonite History,* 51.

[97] Ibid., *57.*

A fourth distinctive, common to most Anabaptist groups, was a sense of community that went beyond mere feeling. Many Anabaptist congregations pooled their goods and re-distributed them to those in need within their body. It was this tendency that often brought forth the worst of the abuses from those outside the movement. It was at Münster that this was done, and the excess of Münster colored the feelings of many. Later groups of Anabaptists, like the Hutterites in Moravia, practiced a very successful communal living.

The importance, in history, of the Anabaptists comes from these common tendencies and their willingness to suffer on their behalf. Anabaptist history contains many stories of persecution and perseverance, for they lived their convictions. Roland Bainton wrote of this important contribution: "The Anabaptists anticipated all other religious bodies in the proclamation and exemplification of three principles which, on the North American continent, are among those truths which we hold to be self-evident: the voluntary church, the separation of church and state, and religious liberty."[98]

A century later, the Quakers followed the same pattern. They began as a protest movement; not of baptism, but of the empty forms and traditions which they found in the Church of England. Like the Anabaptists, they were concerned with a life of commitment that showed real transformation. The nickname "Quaker" comes from the sense of quaking or trembling that

---

[98] Roland Bainton, *Studies on the Reformation* (Boston: Beacon Press, 1963), 199.

Friends produced in those who heard their powerful message. Their actual name was the "Society of Friends," taken from the New Testament verse: "You are my friends if you do what I command" (John 15:14).

In 1647, George Fox began to travel around England, preaching in the markets and at county fairs. He very soon attracted a following that was taken by the message which he proclaimed. Many of those who first joined him were already religious radicals who had been seeking something more than the state church offered. Quakers called people out of the state churches and into a commitment to Christ. The movement began at a great meeting held at Firbank fell, in 1652, as individuals and small groups began to merge together.

These Quakers were very much concerned with the individual's response to God, and they urged individuals to follow the Spirit. They needed no elaborate buildings or programs; their "altar" was in their heart. They needed no baptism or Lord's Supper, because they were baptized in the Holy Spirit and shared daily in the soul's spiritual bread—the living Jesus Christ.[99]

Unlike Anabaptists, they did not put emphasis on baptism. Instead they set the rite of baptism aside looking for a spiritual baptism of the Spirit. They desired to be a spiritual people and urged one another to listen to "that of God within them" and to follow the "inner light of Christ within." This led them away from the strict biblicism which marked the Puritans of their day and which had

---

[99] Arthur Wilford Nagler, *The Church in* History (New York: Abingdon Press, 1929), 180.

also been a part of the Anabaptist movement.

Aside from this, many of the characteristics of the Anabaptists were theirs. Like Anabaptists, they saw the church as voluntary, believing that coercion was unlawful. They refused to pay the tithe to support the state church. They refused to take any oaths. They testified that the church was not to fight, but to suffer. Like the Anabaptists, they were a sharing people; sharing within their own circle with anyone in need and making regular provisions to do so. They also extended their sharing to those who opposed them.

And like the Anabaptists, they suffered persecution. Not a few of them spent considerable time in prison for their beliefs. Like the Anabaptists, they did not fold under this persecution but continued on, and their forbearance has had its impact on history. They lent their support to religious toleration. They influenced many reforms in society—in improving prison conditions, caring for the feebleminded and the infirm, and raising the status of women.

Seventeenth-century Quakers, influenced by many streams of religious thought that preceded them (such as that of the Puritans, Anabaptists, and Collegiants, and the mystical, and holiness movements) continued and expanded the Reformation begun in the sixteenth century. Both Anabaptists and Quakers continue to leave a tremendous legacy behind as people living out their convictions.

Discussion Questions/Projects

1. From the data found in this chapter, compose a two-column chart depicting the similarities and differences between the sixteenth-century Anabaptists and the seventeenth-century Quakers.

2. Both the term Anabaptist and the name Quaker were given to these movements opprobriously. What other religious movements have been branded in a similar way by their opponents? With research find how the term Quaker came into being and what it signifies now.

3. Most people today would recognize the name Mennonite more than they would the term Anabaptist. With some research prepare a short essay describing the main beliefs and practices of Mennonites in the 21st century.

4. Four fundamental tenets of the Friends are found in the expression: "These Quakers were very much concerned with the individual's response to God and they urged individuals to follow the Spirit. They needed no elaborate building or program for their "altar" was in their heart and they needed no baptism or Lord's Supper because they were baptized in the Holy Spirit and shared daily in the soul's spiritual bread—the living Jesus Christ." Compose a short essay elaborating on these four vital beliefs. What is current Friends practice in these four areas?

5. Early Mennonites are known for their diligence in agriculture and for the peace testimony. What distinguished the early Friends? What distinguishes Friends today?

For Further Study

Roland Bainton. *Studies on the Reformation*. Boston: Beacon Press, 1963.

Dyck, Cornelius J. *An Introduction to Mennonite History: A Popular History of the Anabaptists and the Mennonites*. Scottdale: Herald Press, 1981.

Grimm, Harold J. *The Reformation Era, 1500-1650*. New York: Macmillan, 1973.

Harvey, T. Edmund. *The Rise of the Quakers.* London: National Council of Evangelical Free Churches, 1909.

Nagler, Arthur Wilford. *The Church in History.* New York: Abingdon Press, 1929.

Russell, Elbert. *The History of Quakerism.* New York: Macmillan Company, 1943.

Stevenson, William. *The Story of the Reformation*. Louisville: John Knox Press, 1959.

Trueblood, D. Elton. *The People Called Quakers.* Richmond: Friends United Press, 1966.

Walker, Williston. *The Reformation.* New York: Scribner's Sons, 1900.

Williams, Walter. *The Rich Heritage of Quakerism.* Newberg: Barclay Press, 1987.

Mary Fisher 1623-1698

Mary Fisher was a housemaid (an indentured servant) in Yorkshire when she heard George Fox preach. She became a convinced Friend and a member of the Valiant Sixty, carrying the gospel around England, America, and to Turkey.[100]

Having been "convinced of the Truth," Fisher began preaching in Yorkshire between 1652 and 1654. She was imprisoned repeatedly in York for speaking against priests and the hireling ministry. Her stay in the York prison was advantageous for her, however, for there she met three Quakers, Elizabeth Hooton, Jane Holmes, and Thomas Aldam. They took her under their wing, explaining Quaker beliefs and teaching her to read and write.

In the fall of 1653, after her release from prison, she joined Elizabeth Williams in a trip to Cambridge, where the two preached to the seminary students. Because the students were somewhat condemned by the two women's knowledge and use of Scriptures, and because they could not answer them, they became extremely angry. Being rude and mocking, the students called for the constables, and the two women were stripped to the waist and brutally beaten. Once again, Mary was placed in the York prison.

In 1655, she and Ann Austin sailed to Barbados, where they preached with success before sailing up to Boston aboard the *Swallow*. Richard Bellingham, the deputy governor, seized them both, confiscated and burned their Quaker books, and had them

---

[100] Data found at https://www.friendsjournal.org/mary-fisher/ and http://www.quakersintheworld.org/quakers-in-action/187/Mary-Fisher. See also Hodgkin, *A Book of Quaker Saints*, Ch. 28 and Walter Williams, *Rich Heritage of Quakerism*, 67-68.

imprisoned (planning to starve them). They were then sent back to Barbados.

In 1657, she joined a small group of Quakers who set sail from England to take the Truth to Turkey particularly to the Sultan. An English Consul, opposing their plans, had them sent back to Venice. Mary, however, talked the captain into dropping her off on the Greek coast, and from there she trekked alone on to the Sultan's camp outside of Edirne. She gained an audience with the Sultan who received her very well and assured her that he understood her message.

In 1662, Mary married a Friends minister, William Bayle, and at his death (1675), married John Cross. She and John emigrated to Charlestown, South Carolina, where she died in 1698.

Margaret Fell 1614-1702

One cannot read far into the *Journal of George Fox* without meeting up with Margaret Fell. She was the wife of Justice Thomas Fell and the lady of Swarthmoor Hall, in Ulverston, England. Born in 1614, as Margaret Askew, she married Thomas Fell in 1641. Thomas became a Justice of the Peace for Lancashire and was a member of the Long Parliament from 1647 to 1649 when, disapproving of Thomas Cromwell, he quit. She is recognized by many as a founder of the Friends movement and has been called the Nurturing Mother of Quakerism.[101] In 1669, she married George Fox.

In 1652, just after his vision from Pendle Hill, George Fox stopped at Swarthmoor and shared the gospel with Margaret and her children. Fox recorded in his *Journal*: "A convincement of the Lord's truth came upon [Margaret] and her children" and the next day, "the Lord's power seized upon Margaret Fell, her daughter Sarah, and several others."[102] Margaret herself declared, after hearing Fox preaching the next day in the chapel: "this opened me so, that it cut me to the heart, and then I saw clearly we were all wrong. So I sat down in my pew again and cried bitterly: and I cried in my spirit to the Lord."[103]

---

[101] "The Life of Margaret Fell," based on Helen Crosfield, *Margaret Fox of Swarthmoor Hall* (Bishopgate: Headley Bros, 1913). Retrieved from http://www.ushistory.org/penn/margaret_fell.htm

[102] *Journal,* Nickalls, 160, 162.

[103] "The Life of Margaret Fell"

She opened her home, Swarthmoor, to the Friends who were gathering around Fox, and it became a headquarters for the movement. One of the reasons given for the success and growth of Friends was that the movement had someone to "organize and maintain a communication structure that enabled their ministers to evangelize."[104] Margaret Fell was the one who did that for the movement. She wrote letters of encouragement and advice. She kept track of which ministers were where and what their needs were. She offered her home as a place for recuperation. She maintained a fund for financial needs.

She often took pleas on behalf of Friends ministers and for George Fox to King Charles II and to James II. And after her marriage to George Fox in 1669, she collaborated with him to provide the movement with a workable structure. She helped in promoting her husband's ideas and helped establish Women's Meetings.

Like George Fox, Margaret was imprisoned for her preaching and for refusing to take the Oath of Allegiance. She used her prison time to write a number of pamphlets. One significant pamphlet written from prison was her "Women's Speaking Justified."

---

[104] Marjon Ames, *Margaret Fell, Letters, and the Making of Quakerism* (London: Routledge, 2019), 1.

William Penn 1644-1718

William Penn, as a young man, joined the Quaker movement at a time Quakers were under tremendous persecution. He was from a well-to-do family and had strong connections, not only with men in leadership, but also with the king himself. A deep thinker with a religious bent, he had become a defender of religious toleration, even though he was frequently jailed for his belief. From jail, he wrote numerous pamphlets attacking intolerance.

He came to view the Quaker movement as "Primitive Christianity Revived," which was the title of a book published in 1696, in which he described "how the ways of the early Christian church as established by Jesus and his apostles had been restored 'in Faith and Practice of the People called Quakers.'" In that book, or short treatise, he presents the Quaker belief in the reality of "the Light of Christ in Man," a doctrine that distinguished Friends from all other Christians.

Penn proved to be capable of challenging government policies in court, and one of his cases helped secure the right for the jury to be free of the judge. He also used his diplomatic skills and family connections to get large numbers of Quakers out of jail.[105] The land grant given him by the king (in compensation of monies owed his family) was used to create a colony that would champion religious liberty. That colony was Pennsylvania, a "Holy Experiment" established by Penn where everyone "could be free to worship God according to their own conscience." There would be no forts and no

---

[105] Jim Powell, "William Penn, American's First Great Champion for Liberty and Peace," *The Freeman*. Retrieved from http://quaker.org/legacy/wmpenn.html.

soldiers. Native Americans would be paid for the land they relinquished. Prisons would be reformatories.[106] "People would have freedom of speech and trials by juries." All citizens would vote. Elections would be held each year. The constitution for the colony could be amended. [107] According to the Quaker historian, Thomas D. Hamm: "Penn was confident, that if properly constituted, Pennsylvania and its capital, Philadelphia (Greek for 'City of Brotherly Love'), would be a model for the rest of the world." [108]

---

[106] Williams, *Rich Heritage of Quakerism*, 129.

[107] Leonard Kenworthy, *Quakerism: A Study Guide on the Religious Society of Friends* (Dublin: Prinit Press, 1981), 24.

[108] Thomas Hamm, *The Quakers in America* (New York: Columbia University Press, 2003), 27-28.

4
17th-Century Quaker Challenges

1642 The Civil War in England begins.

1646 Puritanism becomes the "official" religion in England.

1647 George Fox begins his ministry.

1649 King Charles I is beheaded.

1649 the beginning of the Commonwealth period

1650 The Blasphemy Act hits Quakers because of their belief in the Inner Light of Christ.

1652 Fox preaches at Firbank Fell beginning the Quaker movement.

1653 the establishment of the Protectorate

1655 George Fox is taken to see Oliver Cromwell.

1657 the voyage of the Woodhouse (Robert Fowler)

1658 Quakers are banned from Plymouth Colony.

1660 the Restoration of the Monarchy with Charles II

1661 The Clarendon Code strikes against all non-conformists.

1662 The Act of Uniformity forcing the Anglican Book of Common Prayer on all people is passed.

1664 The Oath of Allegiance to the king is required of Quakers.

1664 The Conventicle Act disallows any groups of more than five to meet.

1666 The 5th Monarchy plot against Charles II is blamed on Quakers.

The Society of Friends was birthed while England was in the midst of a Civil War. The war between Parliament and King Charles I broke out in 1642, just one year before George Fox began his wandering search for answers in an area adjacent to, if not in the midst of, the warring troops. In 1649, just two years after Fox began his ministry, the war was over, the king was executed (the first such action in England), and a new form of government, a commonwealth (a republican form of government) was established under the leadership of Oliver Cromwell.[109] Civil Wars, experimental governments, and radical changes in leadership tend to bring social unrest and political confusion.

Winning the war was a great victory for the radical Puritans.[110] Although it is difficult to define the Puritan movement, basically, the Puritans were those who wanted to push the Reformation in England to an extreme position[111] and for them the result of the war was a religious revolution. The Church of England (Anglican) was broken up. Presbyterianism[112] and Congregationalism[113] replaced the episcopacy (the religious governance of the Anglican Church). The once powerful Anglican clergy now ministered in secret, like Catholic priests had been forced to do. Intolerance was greatly increased,[114] "severe penalties were

---

[109] There were, in essence, three governments from 1649 to the restoration in 1660. There was first the experimental commonwealth (a national republic) led by Cromwell and then, in 1653, the Protectorate with Cromwell as the Lord Protector, and from 1659 to 1660 Richard Cromwell, son of Oliver, as *de facto* king.

[110] Will Durant and Ariel Durant, *The Story of Civilization: The Age of Louis XIV.* (New York: Simon and Schuster, 1963), 193.

[111] Puritans were part of a reform effort to remove all Roman Catholic elements from the Church of England. Most Puritans wished to remove all ceremonies and practices not rooted in the Bible.

[112] Presbyterianism is a form of church governance with authority invested in a synod of a council of elders.

[113] Congregationalism is a church governing system in which each congregation governs itself.

[114] Durant, 194: "Intolerance was inverted rather than lessened. Instead of

decreed for any criticism of the Calvinistic creed or ritual."[115]

The general persecution of Dissenters, by the Puritans, naturally impacted the Friends. Many were jailed, as Elizabeth Hooton was, for "speaking" to a Puritan minister.[116] Any priest could apply for a warrant against anyone they wished.[117] Because Quakers spoke back to the minister at the conclusion of the sermon; because they met often in large gatherings; because they were outside the church of the majority, having their meetings broken up, being fined, and being placed in jail for the least cause were common experiences of Friends in the eleven years there was no king in England. George Fox in this time was jailed for his refusal to take a position in Cromwell's army.[118]

Friends experienced legislation that was aimed against them. For example, the Blasphemy Act of 1650, which mistakenly considered Ranters and their doctrines the same as early Friends, was designed to wipe out two Ranter doctrines: their understanding of their relationship with God and their belief that immoral acts could be positive religious activities. As John Punshon writes: ". . . one of the Friends' most difficult tasks was to show that . . . Ranterism and Quakerism were not the same thing."[119]

Anglicans persecuting Catholics, Dissenters, and Puritans, the triumphant Puritans, who formerly clamored for toleration, now persecuted Catholics, Dissenters, and Anglicans."

[115] Thomas Macaulay, *History of England from the Accession of James the Second,* as quoted by Durant, 194.

[116] Manners, *Elizabeth Hooton,* 14.

[117] Ibid.

[118] Roberts, George Fox and the Quaker Movement.

[119] Punshon, *Portrait in Grey,* 41.

One author informs us: "In 1656 there were seldom less than one thousand Quakers in prison at one time."[120] They were imprisoned for not paying tithes, for not attending church, for refusing to remove their hats, or for using the singular "thee" instead of the plural "you" when addressing someone of rank. It is reported that "a woman was sent to prison because she had not prevented her husband from allowing a meeting to be held in the house," and another "was fearfully beaten . . . because she reproved a clergyman who had accused her falsely."[121] After the Conventicle Act in 1664, William Dewsberry, an influential Quaker preacher, was imprisoned for saying grace after supper at an inn. He was charged with breaking the act that allowed no more than five people to assemble for worship.[122]

The greatest challenges to Friends came with the Restoration in 1660. Even though Charles II declared his willingness to prevent persecution of the movement, his efforts were spotty and short-lived. Because of their almost continuous gathering together for worship in places other than established chapels, Friends were often accused of meeting to incite plots against the restored monarch, and many Friends were imprisoned. Released from jail, having been charged for plotting against the king, George Fox and Richard Hubberthorne drew up a declaration against plots and fighting and sent it to the press, only to have it taken from

---

[120] Major Douglas, *George Fox: The Red Hot Quaker* (Cincinnati: God's Bible School and Missionary Training Home, 1902), 43. See also Kenworthy, *Quakerism: A Short Guide,* 11. Kenworthy states: "[Because of the] Conventicle Act in 1664 over 2000 Friends were in prison within a year . . . In 1681 there were at least 1000 Quakers in prison and in 1685, approximately 1400."

[121] Douglas, 44.

[122] Ibid.

the press.[123]

George Fox told the story best:[124]

> Upon this insurrection of the Fifth-monarchy-men great havoc was made both in city and country, so that it was dangerous for sober people to stir abroad several weeks after; and hardly could either men or women go up and down the streets to buy provisions for their families without being abused. In the country they dragged men and women out of their houses, and some sick men out of their beds by the legs. Nay, one that was in a fever the soldiers dragged out of his bed to prison; and when he was brought thither he died. His name was Thomas Patching.
>
> Margaret Fell went to the King, and told him what sad work there was in the city and nation, and showed him we were an innocent, peaceable people, and that we must keep our meetings as we used to do whatever we suffered; but it concerned him to see that peace was kept, that no innocent blood might be shed.
>
> Now the prisons everywhere were filled with Friends and others in the city and country, and the posts were so laid for the searching of letters, that none could pass unsearched. We heard of several thousands of our Friends that were cast into prison

---

[123] Fox, *Autobiography*, 195.

[124] Ibid., 195-196.

in several parts of the nation, and Margaret Fell carried an account of them to the King and council. The next week we had an account of several thousands more that were cast into prison, and she went and laid them also before the King and council. They wondered how we could have such intelligence, seeing they had given such strict charge for the intercepting of all letters; but the Lord did so order it that we had an account notwithstanding all their stopping. In the deep sense I had of the grievous sufferings Friends underwent, and of their innocency towards God and man, I was moved to send an epistle to them, as a word of consolation.

Having lost our former declaration in the press, we made haste and drew up another against plots and fighting, got it printed, and sent some copies to the King and council; others were sold up and down the streets, and at the Exchange.

This declaration did somewhat clear the dark air that was over the city and country; and soon after the King gave forth a proclamation that no soldier should search any house without a constable. But the gaols were still full, many thousands of Friends being in prison; which mischief was occasioned by the wicked rising of those Fifth monarchy-men. But when those of them that were taken came to be executed, they did us the justice to clear us openly from having any hand in or knowledge of their plot. After that, the King, being continually importuned thereunto, issued a declaration that Friends should be set at liberty without paying fees. But great labour, travail, and pains were taken before this was obtained; for Thomas Moor and Margaret Fell went often to the King about it.

As the restoration progressed, a number of acts were promulgated by Parliament that impacted Friends dramatically. All citizens were called upon to swear allegiance to the King. This caused Friends, who believed taking any oath was against the word of God, to be imprisoned in great numbers. George Fox spent great time in prison, because he would not swear an oath, and explained many times to magistrates that Christ enjoined his followers not to swear. For Fox, his word could be trusted without an oath. His yes was yes, and his no was no. There are more entries in the Index to the *Autobiography* for oaths than for any other topic.[125]

Challenges also came from legislation passed by Parliament, as it wrestled to take the control of the church out of the King's hands. These acts are referred to as the Clarendon Code even though Edward Hyde, the Earl of Clarendon, and the Lord Chancellor under Charles II, did not personally sponsor the code's four acts. The second and the fourth act are described below. The 1662 Act of Uniformity[126] re-established the Church of England and mandated the use of the revised *Book of Common Prayer* upon everyone. While Friends did not use the book of prayer they could be fined for not doing so. A similar challenge came with the Conventicle Act of 1664 which was designed to prevent the king softening the Act of Uniformity. The act whose full title was an "Act Against Seditious Conventicles" forbade any group of "five or more persons,

---

[125] Fox, Autobiography, 416.

[126] Cross, *Shorter History of England*, 364. See also Hall, *A History of England and the Empire-Commonwealth*, 261-262.

exclusive of members of a family, to hold meetings for religious worship where the Established forms were not used."[127] This directly impacted Quakers as they met city by city in fields and orchards. One historian suggests: "Quakers seem to have been the chief sufferers"[128] because the Clarendon Code was "designed to cripple the Dissenters."[129] George Fox, in his *Journal*, recorded numerous times he and others with him had meetings broken up by the magistrates and were arrested, despite Fox's argument that the act aimed only at seditious meetings and the Friends were in no way seditious people. He wrote a published declaration: ". . . showing from the preamble and terms of the Act that we were not such a people, nor our meetings such as described in that Act."[130]

Friends finally received official sanction after the establishment of the constitutional monarchy of William and Mary. William, the new monarch, believed that the State had no right to determine the way citizens might choose to worship. In 1689, a Toleration Act had been enacted that did not repeal the established laws but suspended them for those who did not participate in the Established Church and who attended other places of worship. This was contingent upon their ascribing to a declaration against transubstantiation and making an oath of allegiance to the king. Because Quakers refused to take oaths a special Quaker Act was added to the Toleration Act, allowing them to hold meetings undisturbed by signing the declaration against transubstantiation, making a confession of Christian beliefs, and promising fidelity to

---

[127] Cross, 365.

[128] Ibid.

[129] *Encyclopedia Britannica Online*, s.v. "Clarendon Code."

[130] Fox, *Autobiography*, 275-276.

the government.[131]

Walter Williams notes: "One of the outstanding characteristics of early Friends was a sense of mission."[132] They acted on this as George Fox noted, by "spreading themselves in the service of the Gospel" not only to all of England, but across the channel to the continent and across the seas to America.[133] Two of the first to reach the Americas were Mary Fisher and Ann Austin, who arrived in Barbados in the West Indies late in 1655.[134] After fruitful ministry in Barbados, these two women went on north to Boston in 1657. There their baggage was searched, their Quaker books were burned, they were imprisoned with little to nourish them, and then they were sent back to Barbados. The Puritans in Boston were "bitterly opposed" to Quakers, believing them to be "blasphemers, heretics, law-breakers, and rebels against government."[135] This strong antipathy to Quakers was increased when, just two days after Fisher and Austin were sent back, Richard Smith, from Long Island, who had become a Quaker in 1654 while in England, arrived in Boston at the same time a ship load of Quakers entered Boston Bay. Again, their baggage was searched especially for "erroneous books and hellish pamphlets," and the ship's captain was forced to take them back to England. Richard Smith was sent back to Long Island by sea lest he "infect" anyone he might meet by travelling by land.[136]

---

[131] Cross, 424-425.

[132] Williams, *Rich Heritage of Quakerism,* 5.

[133] Ibid.

[134] Ibid., 65.

[135] Ibid., 66. See also Bacon, 27.

[136] Bacon, 27.

In order to prevent further invasions of Quakers the great court of Massachusetts passed laws against Quakers. Shipmasters bringing Quakers to Massachusetts would be fined. Anyone owning or concealing a Quaker book would be fined. Any Quaker banished from the colony that might return would be whipped and confined. Returning a third time would mean death.[137]

Friends, however, in their zeal to obey the call of the Lord to spread the Truth were not deterred by these measures. In 1657, a Yorkshire shipbuilder, a Quaker, Robert Fowler, was finishing a new boat. It was his own design and one in which he hoped he would be able to make a tour of the Mediterranean, but all along, as he worked on its construction, he repeatedly heard the Lord speaking to him, that the ship was to be used in the service of Truth. Once the ship, christened the *Woodhouse*, was launched it made its maiden voyage to London where Quaker friends convinced him to follow the Lord's promptings and the Lord's repeated message *"Thou hast her not for nothing."* Robert then agreed to take eleven Friends on to Boston, and the *Woodhouse* left England June 3, 1657 and landed in New Amsterdam on July 31.[138]

The voyage of the *Woodhouse* was a remarkable one. The ship was too small to safely or effectively cross the Atlantic.[139] It had no navigational equipment. What Fowler and the Quakers did have

---

[137] Ibid., 29, 31.

[138] Ibid., 27-30; Vipont, *Story of Quakerism,* 64-66; Hodgkin. *A Book of Quaker Saints*, 283-300; David Klein, "Noah Knew a Thing or Two, Part Nine," *Motor Boating Magazine* 68, no. 3 (September 1941), 10; "Voyage of the Woodhouse," Quaker Tapestry. https://www.quaker-tapestry.co.uk/panel/voyage-of-the-woodhouse/.

[139] Jnana Hodson, "The Woodhouse Mission," Orphan George. Last Modified April 13, 2013. https://jmunrohodson.wordpress.com/2013/04/13/the-woodhouse-mission/

was an unquenchable conviction that the Lord had called them into the service of the Truth and that the Lord would guide them. And he did. Chased by a man-o-war, caught in storms, sailing blind as it were, they prayed daily and let the Lord lead them. In the words of Robert Fowler:

> The Lord God fulfilled His promise . . . we were brought to ask counsel of the Lord and the word was from Him:—"Cut through and steer your straightest course and mind nothing but Me," . . . and He Himself met with us, and manifested Himself largely unto us . . . [so that we] were carried far above storms and tempests, . . . [and we saw] the Lord leading our vessel even as it were a man leading a horse by the head . . . .

The *Woodhouse* deposited the Friends missionaries in New Amsterdam and they faithfully carried Truth to Boston and New England, even though they were persecuted (and several were killed). Besides those who came on the *Woodhouse* in 1657, many others gave their lives. In an entry in his *Journal* for the year 1661, George Fox noted: "And a sad time it was of persecution, but Friends stood nobly in the Truth and valiant for the Lord's name; and at last the Truth came over all."[140] This was at the same time that they heard, in England, that New England had passed a law banishing all Quakers and that several Friends, who had returned to New England, had been hanged and that many in prison waited the same fate.[141]

---

[140] Fox, *Journal*, Nickalls, 411,

[141] Ibid.

One of those in New England killed in 1661 was Mary Dyer. Mary and her husband, William, were members of a Puritan Church in Boston, the same congregation where Anne Hutchinson worshipped. In 1637, when Anne was banished from the church, as she walked out of the building, Mary Dyer, taking her hand, walked out with her. Shortly after, the Dyers went to England (1652-1657) where they became convinced Friends, and, returning to Rhode Island, Mary Dyer served as the nucleus for an ever-growing Friends population. In 1661, stirred by the intolerance in Boston, Mary returned to that city about the same time as William Robinson and Marmaduke Stevenson.[142] All three went to test the law and to declare Truth. All three were hanged.[143]

Seventeenth-century Friends were able to endure prison, to meet again after their meetings were broken up, and to go back to areas where they were banned because they had learned to live in the power of God. They knew experientially that they were called "to turn people from darkness to light that they might receive Christ Jesus," "to turn people to the grace of God," to direct people to the Spirit." [144] The Lord's power had sounded, and they had responded and accepted the power in which they then went forth. A common expression used by Friends and found often in Fox's *Journal* was that "they were moved by the Lord." They knew to live "in the power of the Lord God of heaven and earth, [that made] all nations to tremble and to quake." They were "obedient to his will singly" and willing to receive "the pure wisdom, counsel, and instruction

---

[142] Bacon, 31; Williams, 666; Vipont, 64.

[143] William Robinson (27 October 1659), Marmaduke Stevenson (27 October 1659), Mary Dyer (1 June 1660), and a fourth, William Leddea (14 March 1661).

[144] Fox, *Autobiography*, 14.

from God."[145]

William Penn, in his *A Brief Account of the Rise and Progress of the People Called Quakers* (1694) explained the ability of the Friends to face and overcome the challenges of the century: "They no sooner felt his power and efficacy upon their souls, but they gave up to obey him in a testimony to his power, and with resigned wills and faithful hearts, through all mockings, contradictions, beatings, prisons, and many other jeopardies that attended them for his blessed name sake."[146]

In addition to persecution, there were other challenges that the Friends met in this century. There was the challenge of organization, especially as the movement grew in number. There was the challenge of capturing the beliefs and understandings of the movement so that there could be uniformity of thought. And there was the challenge of assuring Friends would be able to continue to advance, especially in the New World.

Persecution tended to form Friends into a cohesive group. Friends were known for their loyalty for each other and for their concern for others. But the longevity of the persecution put many under severe strain and the growing numbers stretched the unity at times. Some unsettled Friends tended to excesses.[147] One such was James Nayler, a respected leader among Friends, who allowed some men and women to mount him on a horse and enter into the

---

[145] These words are taken from the letter of advice from George Fox to Oliver Cromwell in 1655. Found in George Fox, *The Journal of George Fox,* rev. ed., John Nickalls, ed. (Cambridge: Cambridge University Press, 1952).

[146] William Penn, *The Rise and Progress of the People Called Quakers* (Philadelphia: Friends Book Store, 1870), 18.

[147] Williams, 94.

city of Bristol as if he were Jesus entering Jerusalem on Palm Sunday.[148] Realizing the necessity of organization and control for the movement, George Fox responded to Nayler's indiscretion by establishing monthly, quarterly, and yearly meetings.[149]

After George Fox was released from Scarborough Prison in the fall of 1666, he began what was to be a two-year journey around England establishing the organizational system that exists still today.[150] In his words:

> Then I was moved of the Lord to recommend the setting up of five monthly meetings of men and women in the city of London, besides the women's meetings and the quarterly meetings, to take care of God's glory, and to admonish and exhort such as walked disorderly or carelessly, and not according to truth. For whereas Friends had only quarterly meetings, now truth was spread and Friends grown more numerous, I was moved to recommend the setting up of monthly meetings throughout the nation. The Lord opened to me what I must do, and how the men's and women's monthly and quarterly meetings should be ordered and established in this and other nations . . .[151]

---

[148] Ibid.; Vipont, 57.

[149] Bacon, 22.

[150] Williams, 93; Vipont, 97. Williams states that this was a four-year process.

[151] Fox, *Autobiography*, 254, 335. George Fox explains the reasons for the monthly meetings as being "for looking after the poor, taking care for orderly proceedings in marriages, and other matters relating to the Church of Christ."

This establishment of monthly meetings where the local Friends could encourage and counsel each other, and quarterly meetings, where Friends from a number of monthly meetings, could do the same on a wider scale and consider questions beyond the scope of the local meetings, were aided by the yearly meetings where members of each monthly meeting gathered for spiritual renewal, training, and consideration of even greater concerns. But this was only a portion of the organization of the movement. Margaret Fell, along with her daughters, made her home in Swarthmoor a Friends communication center. Letters expressing appreciation and encouragement or with needed support were sent out regularly to all the publishers of truth. Swarthmoor also became a base or a resting and sending center as well.[152] In addition, several funds were established to provide for those on the road as they spread the gospel and to provide funds for families whose breadwinner might be in prison. The most known of these funds was the Kendal Fund managed by Margaret Fell at Swarthmoor Hall.[153]

Common understanding of the Quaker way became available as the movement found an apologist who was able to "establish Quaker thinking within the context of the Quaker faith."[154] That apologist was Robert Barclay, a young man from Scotland who became a convinced Friend through the ministration of his father's cellmate in the Edinburgh Castle. Robert's father, Colonel David Barclay, had been imprisoned in 1665 because he had held office in the Commonwealth. His cellmate, John Swinton, was a Quaker

---

[152] D. Elton Trueblood, *The People Called Quakers* (Richmond: Friends United Press, 1976), 23; Williams, 58. See also "Quaker History." Last Modified May 3, 2020. http://quaker.org/legacy/ovym/index_files/qhistory.html

[153] Vipont, 44-45, 61; Williams, 90-91, 41, 49, 59.

[154] Ibid., 72.

who introduced the colonel and his son, who often visited, to the Quaker faith. In 1676 Robert Barclay published, *Apology for the True Christian Divinity, being an Explanation and Vindication of the Principles and Doctrines of the People Called Quakers,*[155] otherwise known as *Barclay's Apology.* In this volume, he "stressed the Quaker conception of religion as a living experience, a universal redemption, a Light, Grace, and Seed . . . which is Christ Jesus."[156] In fifteen propositions, Barclay made a systematic presentation of the essential Friends beliefs allowing for the intellectual formation and defense of the Quaker faith.[157]

A final challenge the Friends faced in the seventeenth century was the challenge of continuance when persecution was so relentless. In 1666, during the most difficult days of the persecution, William Penn joined the Friends. William Penn, like Barclay, was from a well-to-do family and had strong connections, not only with men in leadership, but also with the king himself. He became a defender of religious toleration in England, even though he was frequently jailed. From jail he wrote numerous pamphlets attacking intolerance. He proved to be capable of challenging government policies in court, and, in one of his cases, even helped secure the right for the jury to be free of the judge.

Penn used his diplomatic skills and family connections to get large numbers of Quakers out of jail.[158] He used the land grant given him

---

[155] The title of the *Apology* has varied with various editions. Two other titles used have been *Apology for the True Christian Divinity, as the same set forth and preached by the People in Scorn Called Quakers,* and *Barclay's Apology for the True Christian Divinity as Professed by the People Called Quakers.*

[156] Vipont, 113.

[157] Trueblood, 62.

[158] Powell, "William Penn."

by the king (in compensation of monies owed his family) to create a colony that would champion religious liberty. That colony was Pennsylvania.

Discussion Questions/Projects

1. Early in the seventeenth century, Puritans, wanting to remove all vestiges of popery from the church, broke with the Church of England. One group of these left England and founded the colony of Plymouth in the new world. Prepare a short paper describing the Puritans especially their concepts of daily life.

2. Describe, in a short paper, the differences between the Presbyterian and the Congregational systems of church governance. Which system predominates in American churches today? What other patterns now exist?

3. The text includes a biography of Elizabeth Hooton. Prepare a similar biography for one of these early Friends women: Mary Dyer, Ann Austin, Sarah Gibbons, Mary Weatherhead, or Dorothy Waugh.

4. How did the theological beliefs of the Ranters and the Friends compare and contrast? Why would Quakers be confused for Ranters?

5. Were the reasons Friends were imprisoned always valid? How did Friends accept the prison sentences that they received?

6. What two places in the New Testament are we taught not to swear oaths? Why did Jesus give this instruction?

7. Would you be willing to accept time in prison for refusing to take an oath? Do you have convictions that you will not compromise?

8. Two of the Clarendon Codes are mentioned in the text. What were the other two? How did Charles II feel about these codes and the reason they were enacted? Did it change his efforts to have Friends released from jail?

9. There are several acts that are referenced as the "Quaker Act." For example, the Clarendon Codes are sometimes called this because they targeted Quakers. However, the addition to the Toleration Act of 1689 usually bears this title. Why? What did this "Quaker Act" do for Friends?

10. Why did Friends attempt to infiltrate New England? Do we have 20th-century examples of the same kind of missionary endeavors?

11. What do you think of the fact that Puritans sought freedom from the beliefs of the established Church of England, yet persecuted Quakers and others who did not believe as they did?

12. Do research on the voyage of the Woodhouse in order to expand what is included in the text. What would you have done were you in the position Robert Fowler was?

13. The concluding remarks for the chapter rely on a number of expressions taken from the *Journal of George Fox*. Find an electronic copy of the *Journal* and search for instances of these kinds of expressions. How often did George Fox include these explanations in the *Journal*? (If you cannot find an electronic copy that can be searched you might find a copy with a good index.)

For Further Study

Bacon, Margaret. *The Quiet Rebels: The Story of the Quakers in America.* New York: Basic Books, 1969.

Barbour, Hugh and Arthur Roberts. *Early Quaker Writings 1550-1700.* William Eerdmans Publishing Company, 1973.

Davies, Norman. *The Isles: A History.* Oxford: Oxford University Press, 1999.

Douglas, Major. *George Fox: The Red-Hot Quaker.* Cincinnati: God's Bible School and Missionary Training Home, 1902.

Durant, Will and Ariel. *The Story of Civilization: The Age of Louis XIV.* New York: Simon and Schuster, 1963.

Cross, Arthur Lyon. *A Shorter History of England and Great Britain.* New York: Macmillan, 1939.

Fox, George. *The Autobiography of George Fox from His Journal.* Edited by Henry Stanley Newman. London: S. W. Partridge and Company, 1886.

Hall, Walter Phelps, Robert Greenhalgh Abion and Jennie Barnes Pope. *A History of England and the Empire-Commonwealth.* Boston: Blaisdell Publishing, 1961.

Manners, Emily. *Elizabeth Hooton: First Quaker Woman Preacher (1600-1672). London: Headley Bros., 1914*

Punshon, John. *Portrait in Grey: A Short History of the Quakers.* 2nd Ed. Fitchburg: Quaker Books, 2006.

Roberts, Arthur. "George Fox and the Quaker (Friends) Movement." Retrieved from https://www.georgefox.edu/about/history/quakers.html

Vipont, Elfrida. *The Story of Quakerism, 1652-1952.* Richmond: Friends United Press, 1977.

Williams, Walter. *The Rich Heritage of Quakerism.* Newberg: Barclay Press, 1987.

William "Irish Hammer" Edmundson 1627-1712

William Edmundson heard of the Quakers well before he met one and he was intrigued and delighted with what he heard. He records in his *Journal* (for 1651) that when the Parliamentary Army troop he was a member of was quartered in Derbyshire and Chesterfield:

> ...the common discourse of all sorts of people was of the Quakers, and various reports were of them the priests everywhere were angry against them, and the baser sort of people spared not to tell strange stories of them; but the more I heard of them the more I loved them, yet had not the opportunity to speak with any of them.[159]

William had that opportunity, sometime later in 1653, when he crossed over from Ireland to England on business and found George Fox and James Nayler having a meeting a short distance from where he was. Having the opportunity to converse with the people he had a love for and believed in, he and his two companions were "convinced of the Lord's blessed Truth, for God's witness in our hearts answered to the Truth of what was spoken, and the Lord's former dealing with me came fresh in my remembrance. Then I knew it was the Lord's hand that had been striving with me for a long time."[160]

His understanding began to be opened, Scriptures that he did not understand before now made sense to him, and he began to be obedient to the Truth he had received. In a memorial for him at his

---

[159] William Edmundson, *The Journal of the Life, Travels, and Suffering of the Labour of Love in the Work of Ministry of that Worthy Elder and Faithful Servant of Jesus Christ William Edmundson* (London: Mary Hindi, 1774), 7, 11. Retrieved from https://archive.org/details/journaloflifetra00inedmu/.

[160] Ibid., 8.

death, one said of him, "He was a man of uncommon courage, and the Truth Invigorating his understanding, made him as bold as a lion; he was early convinced of the everlasting Truth, and soon was publicly engaged in its service." His nickname "Irish Hammer" came from his powerful declaration of the Word. It fell like the blows of a hammer on needy souls. He took the Quaker message to Ireland. He formed the first recorded Meeting for Worship in Lurgan, County Armagh in 1664.[161]

He accompanied George Fox to Barbados and America in 1671, and then returned to preach in Virginia and the West Indies at least twice after that. While in America in 1662 Edmundson joined Friends in a debate of fourteen propositions in a challenge from Roger Williams. The propositions turned out to be only "slanders and accusation against Quakers" and they were all turned back upon him so that the people saw his "weakness, folly, and envy against the Truth and Friends."[162] Edmundson penned a letter of advice to Friends in America calling them to free their slaves. Some consider this to be the first Quaker voice raised regarding this issue.

---

[161] Gravestone inscription. Retrieved from https://www.findagrave.com/memorial/105236758/william-edmundson.

[162] Edmundson, 74.

5
Quakers in the 18th century

1676 West Jersey established as Quaker colony
1681 Pennsylvania established as a Holy Experiment
1689 The Toleration Act
1702 Quakers lose control of West Jersey.
1715 early Pennsylvania 'minute' against slavery
1756 Friends withdraw from the Pennsylvania Assembly
    rather than support the French and Indian War.
1758 Slave Trading is made illegal in Quaker colonies.
1761 London Yearly Meeting 'minute' against slave trading
1775 Pennsylvania Abolition Society founded
1775 the outbreak of the American Revolution
1776 the Declaration of Independence
1781 The Society of free Quakers is formed.
1787 Society for the Effecting of Abolition of the Slave
    Trade is founded.
1789 The United States Constitution is adopted.
1795 Baltimore Yearly Meeting appoints an Indian Affairs
    Committee.

Margaret Fell Fox, William Edmundson, and William Penn were the exceptions; very few of the leaders of the first generation of Friends made it into the eighteenth century. Robert Barclay died in 1690; George Fox the next year in 1691. Thus, the Friends began the new century without their most notable leadership.

The persecution in England was over; Friends under the Toleration Act of 1689 could now worship unhindered. In America, Quakers in the middle and southern colonies could as well; those in most of

New England were still not tolerated.

As Friends entered the eighteenth century, the excitement of the first half century diminished and official acceptance seemed to have lessened the enthusiasm of evangelism. Friends were now more concerned to avoid the excessive enthusiasm and actions that had caused persecution in the past; instead they focused on disciplining their own membership and tightly overseeing their meetings.[163] Quaker historians Howard Brinton and Elfrida Vipont both suggest that Friends moved to a position of conservatism: "from a loosely-knit fellowship to a more structured religious society."[164] The practice of disowning those who did not measure up was begun.[165]

Because the first Friends had placed their focus on evangelism and training those ministers who were traveling, they did not seem to be concerned with educating the second generation. The religious values which would have had to have been transmitted to the children were not automatically caught by the second generation.[166] It was not until 1667, twenty years into the

---

[163] Bacon, *Quiet Rebels*. 43; Williams, *Rich Heritage of Quakerism*, 109. Williams speaks of the Friends movement just after the Toleration Act as "at spring tide." While he does not speak of the declension as boldly as Bacon does, his introduction to the century indicates the same.

[164] Howard Brinton, *Friends for 300 Years* (Wallingford: Pendle Hill Publications, 1972), p. 181. Brinton states: "No religious movement has ever maintained the fire, energy and power which accompanied its formative period." The summary of Vipont is from Kenworthy, *Quakerism,* 23. Kenworthy notes that "Some of the original zest of the movement lingered well into the 18th century on both sides of the Atlantic Ocean and the totality of the Quaker message and mission remained intact."

[165] Bacon, 42.

[166] Bacon, 42.

movement, that Fox recommended the establishment of schools.[167] Consequently, although many of this second generation did "inherit the intense group loyalty which outside persecution had developed among their parents," they lacked "the radiant spirit which made these first Friends missionaries advance to the far corners of the earth." [168] Rather than be rebuffed by the world, as their parents had been, the children of the first generation preferred to keep carefully separate. In the words of one historian, although itinerant ministers kept the authentic Quaker message alive: ". . . the days of the great preachers and the large public meetings were gone and the evangelistic fervor of the early days of the movement was lacking."[169] William Braithwaite recorded: "It must be confessed that the Quaker movement . . . was resting on its past, accommodating itself to the ease of the present, and losing its vision."[170]

A great migration of Friends in the late 1680's and early 90's saw many Friends emigrate from England to America. In 1682 a ship, the *Welcome*, dropped anchor off the shore of Delaware with 270[171] Quaker passengers bound for Delaware and Pennsylvania.

---

[167] Fox, *Journal*, Nickalls, 461.

[168] Bacon, 42. Howard Brinton says something similar: "Most of the first leaders had died, many of them in prison, and a second generation coming on who were not motivated by the blinding fire and acute zeal that comes from the discovery of a new truth or from resistance to violent opposition." Brinton, 182.

[169] Kenworthy, 27.

[170] William Braithwaite. *The Second Period of Quakerism* (New York: MacMillan and Co., 1919), 631. While it may be that Braithwaite is correct it is also true that as Howard Brinton states, "In the transition for the first period to the second, there was no change in doctrine but there was an important change in behavior." Brinton, 182.

[171] 300 had begun the voyage, but 30 died in route.

By the beginning of the eighteenth century there were numerous Quakers in Rhode Island, Delaware, West Jersey, Pennsylvania, and the Carolinas. There were as many as three Yearly Meetings set up in America before 1700.[172]

Friends came to dominate Rhode Island, a colony that was established as a haven for dissenters granting religious freedom to all. About half of the population was Quaker and, for thirty-six terms, the governors of Rhode Island were Quakers. What we know today as New Jersey was land given by Charles II to two British Lords, Lord Berkeley and Sir George Carteret. In 1674, Lord Berkeley sold his share in the colony to some Quakers including Robert Barclay. The colony was then split into two portions. West Jersey owned by the Quakers and East Jersey which, soon after (1682), was purchased by William Penn. This meant that most of the land between Maryland and New York was in Quaker hands. In 1702, however, the two halves were joined into one, New Jersey, and ownership went to an elected assembly which was not controlled by Quakers.[173]

The most known of the Quaker efforts in the New World, is of course, the colony of Pennsylvania. After the death of his father, Admiral William Penn, William Penn not only inherited his father's estates in Ireland, but also the claim for a sizable loan that King Charles II had taken from Penn's father. Charles II was happy to pay this debt by granting to Penn a grant of land between Maryland and New York which became the colony of Pennsylvania. It was an area larger than England and Wales combined and, although Charles

---

[172] Kenworthy, 24.

[173] Martin Kelly, "Founding and History of the New Jersey Colony." Last Modified on June 30, 2019. https://www.thoughtco.com/new-jersey-colony-103874

had no idea of this, it "contained more valuable soil and minerals than any other province of English America."[174] Here Penn established his "Holy Experiment" where everyone "could be free to worship God according to their own conscience." There would be no forts and no soldiers. Native Americans would be paid for the land they relinquished. Prisons would be reformatories.[175] "People would have freedom of speech and trials by juries." All citizens would vote. Elections would be held each year. The constitution for the colony could be amended.[176]

According to the Quaker historian, Thomas D. Hamm: "Penn was confident, that if properly constituted, Pennsylvania and its capital, Philadelphia (Greek for 'City of Brotherly Love'), would be a model for the rest of the world."[177]

There were several consequences that came from the migration of Quakers to West Jersey or Pennsylvania from England. The numbers leaving England included the young and the able and left an older generation behind.[178] The largest number of Friends changed

---

[174] Alan Brinkley, *American History: A Survey*, 11th ed. (New York: McGraw-Hill, 2003), 52-54.

[175] Williams, 129.

[176] Kenworthy, 24.

[177] Thomas Hamm, *The Quakers in America* (New York: Columbia University Press, 2003), 27-28.

[178] Donna Hay, "Quakers in Great Britain: 1652-1750s. https://haygenealogy.com/hay/quaker/quaker-GB.html: "Prior to the mass exodus of Quakers from England to America in the 1680s and 1690s, it is estimated that the Quaker population hit a high of over 60,000 members, or 1% of the total population of Great Britain. This fell off dramatically in the next decades, and by 1806 the total number of Quakers in England was halved to 32,000, while by 1883 this had dwindled further to 15,219, (with just 193 in Scotland). Conversely in America in 1883 the Quaker population was estimated

from England to the Americas. As Quakers in America also migrated from one colony to another, they tended to take their culture with them. This migration within the colonies helped establish a homogeneous Quaker culture that was careful to preserve the traditions of the first generation and to add elements that would make them distinctive. Thus, a centrality of the Spirit, silent waiting upon the Spirit in worship, honesty, diligence in business, use of thee and thou instead of you, the refusal to take oaths or to participate in war, and the participation of women in ministry were fastidiously retained.[179] Added were distinctive characteristics in dress.

Their growing singularities of dress,[180] included the wearing of "Quaker gray, the broad-brimmed hat, and the Quaker bonnet."[181] Friends attempted to dress plainly and not use bright colors or the latest styles. Instead they chose a somber gray color and their clothing had no ornamentation. However, the material, itself, was often the best most durable quality. In fact, the longer the practice of uniform clothing lasted, the higher quality it became. Yet, not all Friends welcomed a common Quaker costume. Margaret Fell, for example in 1700 said:

> ...Christ Jesus saith, that we must take no thought what we shall eat, or what we shall drink, or what we shall put on; but bids us consider the lilies how they grow in more royalty than Solomon. But contrary to this, they say we must look at no colours,

---

at six times as large as that in England: 90,000-100,000."

[179] Kenworthy, 26.

[180] This is the expression used by William Braithwaite, *Second Period of Quakerism*, 459.

[181] Bacon, 43.

nor make anything that is changeable colours as the hills are, nor sell them nor wear them. But we must be all in one dress, and one colour. This is a silly poor Gospel. [182]

But whether to dress plainly or not was not the major question that Friends faced in the eighteenth century. As the Holy Experiment was being fleshed out in the colony of Pennsylvania, Friends serving on the Assembly were faced with a daily dilemma. The crown demanded that monies be raised in each colony for defense. Friends in Pennsylvania, because of their peaceful relations with the Native Americans, believed no defenses were needed. They did not rush to the fortifications when Native Americans came around. They did not carry arms. So, should they comply and raise monies for soldiers and arms? Or should they remain true to their Quaker principles, and disobey the demand and not raise funds? Could they raise monies for the crown for other purposes even though they were certain it would be used not for the purpose they earmarked it but for defense?

Then the outbreak of the French and Indian War[183] forced a decision. Friends realized that they could not participate in the governing process of the colony as that meant being party to waging war. Since the war began on the borders of Pennsylvania, they could not just ignore it. Thus, in 1756, the majority of Friends serving on the Assembly resigned. Friends began to retreat into

---

[182] Bill Samuel, "Quakerism in the 18th Century, http://www.quakerinfo.com/quak_18.shtml. See also Vipont, 134.

[183] The French and Indian War was not a war between the French and the Native Americans but, rather, the French and Native Americans against the English. The war, also known as the Great War for Empire or the Seven-Years' War ran from 1756 to 1763.

separatism. However, they could not isolate themselves completely and so continued to face challenges of paying war taxes, providing material that could be used in war, and whether or not to support the newly-formed Continental Congress that promoted war once the decision had been made to seek independence from Britain. The American Revolution became an extremely testing time for Friends, both in America and in Britain who faced the same dilemma of being part of a nation at war.[184]

The resignation of Quakers from the political leadership in Pennsylvania is seen by some as the turning point for Friends in the eighteenth century. Up to 1756, Friends were active in their world, and in Pennsylvania, at least, attempting to put their principles to work in public affairs. After 1756, Friends moved away from the world separating them from the mainstream of activity to be the peculiar people that the Quaker gray projected.[185] Others believe that the retreat into separateness began as early as 1689 and that a period of Quietism characterized Friends from 1690 to 1825.[186]

Margaret Bacon describes Quietism as a "form of mysticism that emphasizes that man, without God is incapable of goodness." Friends must let their reasoning and planning be quiet and suspended so that God can reveal himself and give guidance. Thus, rather than gathering to hear ministers exhort and explain their messages from the Spirit or Scripture, Friends met in silence. Sometimes this was total silence since no one would speak because they were afraid it would be the creature speaking rather than the

---

[184] Arthur Mekeel, "The Relation of the Quakers to the American Revolution," *Quaker History* 65, No.1 (Spring 1976): 3-18.

[185] Bacon, 68.

[186] Williams, 119.

Spirit. Quietism influenced Friends in England, on the Continent, and in America.[187] While this subdued the evangelistic thrust and missionary focus of the movement, out of Quietism came "some of the most beautiful lives of service and self-sacrifice that the Society has ever known..."[188] Howard H. Brinton reminds us that Quietism did not mean inactivity. Instead, he suggests, as they waited in quiet for guidance from the Lord they were "far from quiet once they were assured of the right word or deed. Their period of withdrawal was followed by a return to activity with an increase of insight and power." [189] Friends continued to become "active agents in . . . social reform."[190]

As intimated above, there were many Friends in this quiet period who gave themselves in service. There were Anthony Benezet (1713-1784) and Thomas Chalkley (1675-1741), both of whom were involved in education. Benezet, in addition to teaching, was a writer and an abolitionist. He offered classes for African Americans, and out of his concern that educational opportunities were not available for women he established a school for girls. His teaching methodology centered on personal kindness for all students. Through his efforts, the first Quaker free day school for African Americans was created. He supported financially efforts to abolish slavery and the slave trade. [191] Thomas Chalkley served as a Quaker

---

[187] Bacon, 84 and Williams, 119.

[188] Vipont, 150.

[189] Brinton, 182.

[190] Ibid.

[191] *Encyclopedia Britannica Online*, s.v. "Anthony Benezet;" "Anthony Benezet: 1713-1784. Quakers in the World. http://www.quakersintheworld.org/quakers-in-action/60/Anthony-Benezet

minister, teacher, and abolitionist. In addition, he represented the Friends Meeting in Philadelphia as a missionary to Mennonites in Holland and Germany. Rebeca Jones (1739-1818) joined the Friends as a young girl and became a minister in 1758 at the age of 19. She too, taught for many years and was instrumental in the establishment of the Westtown (Pennsylvania) Boarding School. As a Friends minister she travelled throughout England and there helped establish a women's meeting.[192] Catherine Phillips (1727-1794) in England campaigned for a larger role for women among Friends and helped establish the Women's Yearly Meeting in 1784.

There were others who focused on ministry and abolition. Joshua Evans (1731-1798) was a mason, a Quaker journalist, and a travelling minster who not only lived near John Woolman but also wore undyed clothing and spoke out for abolition. Likewise, David Ferris (1707-1779) from Wilmington, Delaware, gave himself to addressing the issue of slavery among Friends.[193] William Savery (1750-1804) was still another voice for abolition and the rights of Native Americans.[194] In 1798 his message touched the heart of a young girl in England and changed her life. She was Elizabeth Fry who later was a main force in affecting prison reform in England.[195]

---

[192] Laura Takahashi, "Biography - Philadelphia-born Quaker Minister Rebecca Jones 1739-1818." Last Modified March 9, 2013. https://writersdolaundrytoos.blogspot.com/2013/03/biography-philadelphia-born-quaker.html

[193] Martha Paxson Grundy, "David Ferris: Arguments Against Quaker Slaveholding," *Quaker History* 103, no 2 (Fall 2014): 18-29. doi: 10.1353/qkh.2014.0007

[194] "Anti-Slavery: Some Quaker Leaders." Quakers in the World, http://www.quakersintheworld.org/quakers-in-action/97/-Anti-Slavery-Some-Quaker-Leaders

[195] Alice Almond Shrock, "To act in the spirit "not of judgment, but of mercy:"

Samuel Fothergill (1715-1772) as a traveling minister visited much of England and Ireland. In Ireland, he attempted to revive the Quaker movement. He also lived in the colonies for a while, where he worked at reconciling colonists with Native Americans. He also raised support for the poor. Other travelling ministers included three women: Susann Morris (1682-1745), Elizabeth Hudson (1722-1783), and Anne Moore (1710-1783).[196]

An individual in the eighteenth century who epitomized Friends as religious reformers, seeking to change the spirit of life was John Woolman.[197] John Woolman, born in 1720 in New Jersey, deeply felt that "slaveholding was inconsistent with Christianity and spent his life traveling, observing, and advocating against slavery."[198] His labor in this began in 1742, at the age of 22, when he was asked to write up a bill of sale for a slave. The incident is described well by John Greenleaf Whittier:[199]

> In the year 1742, an event, simple and inconsidera-
> ble in itself, was made the instrumentality of exert-
> ing a mighty influence upon slavery in the Society of

Quaker Activist Elizabeth Fry Pioneered a New Approach to Prison Reform," *Christian History*, 117 (2016), 28-32.

[196] Margaret Hope Bacon, *Wilt Thou Go on My Errand?* (Wallingford: Pendle Hill Publications, 1994).

[197] William Braithwaite describes all Quakers in the seventeenth century as "religious reformers seeking to change the spirit of life, rather than political levellers." Braithwaite, *Second Period of Quakerism,* 556.

[198] Anne Moore Mueller, "John Woolman," Quakers and Slavery, http://web.tricolib.brynmawr.edu/speccoll/quakersandslavery/commentary/people/woolman.php.

[199] John Greenleaf Whittier, "Introduction," in *The Journal of John Woolman* (London: Headley Brothers, 1871), 8.

Friends. A small storekeeper at Mount Holly, in New Jersey, a member of the Society, sold a Negro woman and requested the young man in his employ to make a bill of sale of her. On taking up his pen, the young clerk felt a sudden and strong scruple in his mind. The thought of writing an instrument of slavery for one of his fellow-creatures oppressed him. God's voice against the desecration of his image spoke in his soul. He yielded to the will of his employer, but, while writing the instrument, he was constrained to declare, both to the buyer and the seller, that he believed slave-keeping inconsistent with the Christian religion.

After writing that one bill of sale in 1742, Woolman refused to write another. He also refused to write wills that involved the inheritance of slaves. His testimony went further than refusal to write instruments of slavery. He wore only undyed clothing, since dyes were produced by slave labor. He refused hospitality (paying instead) if the hospitality accrued from slavery.

In 1746, Woolman travelled in the South with another Friend on mission. There the conditions under which slaves were forced to live grieved him. He was troubled to see slaveholders enjoying life made possible by slaves, and he was unhappy to receive hospitality from those who held slaves. Back home he wrote an essay, "Some Considerations on the Keeping of Negroes." The essay was not published, however, until 1754. He made a second trip, this time through New England, and on returning he persuaded Friends to request the legislature to abolish the slave trade. He began to visit Quaker ministers and elders urging them one by one to relinquish their slaves. After still another mission to the South he served on a

Yearly Meeting committee that was formed to visit slave holders to persuade them to give up their slaves.[200]

After a period of intense prayer and waiting upon the Lord (Woolman describes it as "a weighty Exercise" that had been laid on him)[201] Woolman spoke at the Philadelphia Yearly Meeting session in 1758 and his words helped convince the Yearly Meeting to eliminate all slave holding. The effect was that in the words of Elfrida Vipont: "Long before Abraham Lincoln was born, The Society of Friends was free from the taint of slavery."[202] Friends did more than just convince those who held slaves to emancipate them; they also "asked slave owners to reimburse their slaves for their time in bondage."[203] Stephen Angell reports: "By 1784 all North American Yearly Meetings officially prohibited slaveholding among their members."[204]

Woolman's concerns were not limited to slavery alone. Each of the social concerns of his day was real to him. He gave opposition to paying taxes for war. He supported young men, the conscientious objectors of his day, who felt they could not participate in war. He realized and urged others to understand that just refusing to support war or refusing to fight was not sufficient. What was needed was living as peacemakers; living in the virtue of that life

---

[200] Bacon, 97-98.

[201] John Woolman, *Journal*, Chapter V
https://www.gutenberg.org/files/37311/37311-h/37311-h.htm

[202] Vipont, 158.

[203] Richard Foster. *Celebration of Discipline*. Harper San Francisco, 1978, p. 158, quoting Rufus Jones, *The Quakers in the American Colonies*. Norton, 1921, p. 517. See John Woolman, *Journal* (London: Headley Brothers, 1871), 119.

[204] Stephen Angell, "Seeking Freedom," *Christian History*, 117 (2016), 25.

and power that took away the occasion of all wars.[205] He showed active concern for Native Americans. He refused to profit from those things created by the disadvantage of others (such as riding a stagecoach that depended on over-worked horses and stage boys).

In his dependence upon the Holy Spirit, his faithfulness to address the needs of his age, his concern for both the oppressed and the oppressor, John Woolman indeed is a fine representation of Friends in the eighteenth century.

---

[205] Vipont, 155.

Discussion Questions/Projects

1. When the excitement of the first generation begins to dim and "the mechanism of organization begins to replace the free activity of the living organism"[206] how can the excitement be brought back to life? What other great movements faced this problem? Does your faith tradition face this today?

2. Beginning with the eighteenth-century Friends and continuing on today education has been a central and important aspect of the movement. Why, do you suppose, education of the second generation did not happen?

3. Friends settled in Pennsylvania, Jersey, and Maryland, but also in Connecticut and Rhode Island as well as the Carolinas. Prepare a geographical map of the colonies indicating on it the areas where Quakers settled and the dates of those settlements. You may have to review the travels of George Fox (from his *Journal*) and other Quakers to do this.

4. Research Penn's "Holy Experiment" in Pennsylvania and make a list of the ways that that colony differed from others. How many of the distinctives stemmed from Quaker beliefs?

5. The expression "a homogeneous Quaker culture" is used in the text. What is your understanding of what that expression means? What makes a culture Quaker?

6. Quaker costume is spoken of in the chapter. What exactly did the "Quaker Gray" costume consist of? How long did the practice of wearing distinctive clothing persist? Should Friends be known for a particular way of dressing today?

7. What was the favorite color of dress for Margaret Fell? Websites for the Quakerranter.org and the Friends Journal should give you help for this.

---

[206] Braithwaite, 32.

8. Surprisingly nothing is mentioned in the text concerning Friends involvement in the First Great Awakening, a spiritual revival which ran from about 1735 to 1745 in all of the colonies of North America. Although the revival mostly impacted Puritan churches what impact did it have on Friends?

9. The French and Indian War 1756-1763 was a dilemma for Friends, especially those in leadership. At age thirty-six John Woolman struggled in a number of ways—should he pay war taxes, could he house soldiers, how could he support young men who by their conscience could not fight? Chapters IV and V of his *Journal* will give you a good sense of the struggle. How did the same kind of questions get answered for Friends in the Revolution, in WWI and II, and for the Vietnam War?

10. Do you consider Friends in the twenty first century to be mystics? Why or why not? In what ways may the Quietist period in Friends history be described as a period of mysticism?

11. Friends in the period of Quietism may not have been as overtly evangelical as those of the first generation, yet the chapter suggests that many of the great reformers among the Friends gave their lives in service to other Friends and the world. Who are the ones referenced here and what kind of service did they give?

12. Nothing is said of the childhood of John Woolman. Check out the stories of his reading Revelation, and the Robin's nest, and the contrition he felt when his father spoke to him of his undutiful conduct towards his mother. See the first chapter of his *Journal*.

13. What do you think were John Woolman's most important methods to convince slave owners to abandon the practice of slavery? The text suggests at least two.

14. In our world today, what are situations in which we can follow John Woolman's practice of refusing to eat sugar processed by slaves, and to wear dyed clothing, because slaves made the dyes?

For Further Study

Angell, Stephen. "Seeking Freedom," *Christian History*, 117 (2016): 24-28.

Bacon, Margaret. *The Quiet Rebels: The Story of the Quakers in America*. New York: Basic Books, 1969.

_____. *Wilt Thou Go on My Errand*? Wallingford: Pendle Hill Publications, 1994.

Beck, William. *George Whitehead; His Work and Service as a Minister for Sixty-eight Years in the Society of Friends*. London: Headly Brothers, 1901.

Braithwaite, William. *The Second Period of Quakerism*. London: MacMillan and Company, 1919.

Brinton, Howard. *Friends for 300 Years*. Wallingford: Pendle Hill Publications, 1972.

Hamm, Thomas. *The Quakers in America*. New York: Columbia University Press, 2003.

Kenworthy, Leonard. *Quakerism: A Study Guide on the Religious Society of Friends*. Dublin: Prinit Press, 1981.

Mekeel, Arthur J. "The Relation of the Quakers to the American Revolution," *Quaker History* 65, No.1 (Spring 1976): 3-18.

Vipont, Elfrida. *The Story of Quakerism, 1652-1952*. Richmond: Friends United Press, 1977.

Whittier, John Greenleaf. "Introduction." In *The Journal of John Woolman*. London: Headly Brothers, 1871.

Williams, Walter R. *The Rich Heritage of Quakerism*. Barclay Press, 1987.

Woolman, John. *The Journal of John Woolman*. London: Headly Brothers, 1871.

George Whitehead 1636-1723

George Whitehead became a Friend at the age of fifteen and, at eighteen, he began to visit prisons. It was in the prison at Norwich in 1654 that he began to minister to and to fellowship with Richard Hubberthorne, a Quaker minister and member of the Valiant Sixty. Before the year was out, Whitehead was in prison with him.[207] In fact, George Whitehead spent most of his teenage years in prison for his faith.

Whitehead was a very active member of the Valiant Sixty and continued his ministry among Friends for sixty-eight years before his death in 1723. After the death of George Fox in 1691, Whitehead took on a leadership role among Friends. He had a keen mind and was an able presenter of Friends beliefs. In 1662, he was one of four men who pled the cause of Friends before the House of Commons as they considered a bill to prevent nonconformists to hold worship services. In his lifetime, he represented Friends before four different kings—Charles II, James II, William III, and George I.[208]

George Whitefield was so often in prison that he took up the practice of carrying his nightcap in his pocket when he went to meeting so that he would be prepared to spend the night in jail. [209] One time George Whitehead was put in prison for praying in public. When the judge told him he could go free if he paid twenty pounds he replied: "I cannot pay any fine or money for praying to God or worshipping him; and as for promising to cease attending meetings

---

[207] Williams, *Rich Heritage of Quakerism*, 56.

[208] Ibid., 112.

[209] Ibid.

there, I am not my own. I stand in the will of God, neither can I promise any such thing as to restrict coming to worship or pray to God."[210]

Whitehead is remembered for his representative work on behalf of Quakers to the kings of England and his writings. In 1692 he published an influential book, *Antichrist in Flesh Unmasked,* in which he gave a very clear account of the beliefs of Friends.[211] His Journal, *The Christian Progress of George Whitehead,* also very clearly stated the need to die to self on the cross and to be totally committed to Jesus Christ.[212]

---

[210] Susanna Laird, "Lesson About George Whitehead." Last Modified on September 16, 2017. https://www.fgcquaker.org/cloud/frederick-friends/fds/resources/lesson-about-george-whitehead

[211] Williams, 69.

[212] Hall Worthington, "The Christian Progress of George Whitehead," The Missing Cross to Purity. https://www.hallvworthington.com/Whitehead/ChristianProgress.html

6
19th-Century Friends

```
1790-1830 the Second Great Awakening
1812-1815 The War of 1812 impacts the newly formed
United States as the Napoleonic wars slow down in Europe.
1827-1828 the Great Separation
1830-1840 the Charles G. Finney revivals
1830 Joseph Smith founds the Church of Latter Day Saints.
1845 the Wilbur/Gurney separations in New England
1854 the Wilber/Gurney separations in Ohio
1861-1865 the American Civil War
1887 The Richmond Declaration
```

If there is one single word that best characterizes Friends in the nineteenth century it would be, unfortunately, the word "divided." Friends were divided by whether they chose to participate in war and to support war efforts or not. For Friends in England and on the Continent, this was over the Napoleonic Wars that impacted most of Europe from 1800 to 1815. For American Friends, it involved the War of 1812 (1812-1815), the Mexican American War (1846-1848), and the American Civil War (1861-1865).

Friends also became divided, at least in the United States, over the issue of slavery previous to the Civil War; some Friends were certain that others went too far in their abolitionist stance. For a period of time Indiana Yearly Meeting was divided into two Yearly Meetings; one of which was the Anti-Slavery Yearly Meeting. Before the nineteenth century ended, Friends, both in Europe and in America, were divided over theology and practice. These divisions split the movement between orthodox and Hicksite camps and between Gurneyite and Wilburite factions.

The nineteenth century was a turbulent time of change. Not one, but two distinct phases[213] of the Industrial Revolution created new mores, new lifestyles, and many social issues which became concerns for Friends.[214] Changes in industry, in transportation, and in communication were revolutionary. The industrial changes moved people to the cities and often caused differences between city Friends and country Friends. Canals and railroads increased contacts among people, changing the way people lived and worked, but also bringing along a number of social ills. Early in the nineteenth century, the Second Great Awakening brought revival and reform movements to the States, but also brought challenges to Christianity in the creation of new forms of religion. These changes, which should have furthered unity, instead brought division.

To tell the story of Friends in this century, one will need to examine three themes: Friends and war, Friends and social issues (especially slavery and the treatment of prisoners and the mentally ill), and the actual divisions that happened within the Friends movement.

Early in the century, the Napoleonic wars raged in Europe and spilled over into the newly formed United States in the War of

---

[213] The first Industrial Revolution ran from about 1750 to 1850, with the "Second Industrial Revolution" running from 1850 to 1914.

[214] Wilmer A. Cooper states this well: "[Friends] developed philanthropic work in prisons, in care for the insane, and in efforts to offset the ill effects of the Industrial Revolution on workers and their families." See, Wilmer Cooper. *A Living Faith; an Historical and Comparative Study of Quaker* Beliefs, 2nd ed. (Richmond, Friends United Press, 2006), 4-5. Margaret Bacon defines the Friends use of the term concern as being so troubled by an issue that one feels a duty to act. See Margaret Bacon, *Quiet Rebels,* 122.

1812. Mid-century the United States declared war on its neighbor Mexico. And, for American Friends, the American Civil War was an extremely trying time. All three wars impacted Friends whose historic peace testimony had been stated in a declaration given to King Charles II in 1660:[215]

> We utterly deny all outward wars and strife and fightings with outward weapons, for any end or under any pretense whatsoever. And this is our testimony to the whole world.

This stand caused Quakers to be caught between official state policies and their beliefs, especially in the War of 1812. Friends in the States were accused of being friendly with the British; Friends in Canada were accused of being friendly to Americans.[216] Although good loyal citizens, Friends were questioned and mistrusted because of their peace testimony and their quiet opposition to the war activities of the government as well as their readiness to help any who was in need including the British.[217]

In 1812 some went to great lengths to avoid contributing to war. Historian Donald G. Anger records how "One Quaker . . . took his wagon apart down to its wood and nails so as to avoid having to

---

[215] Sandra McCann Fuller, "A Parcel of Quakers and the War of 1812-14 in Upper Canada," *Canadian Quaker History Journal* 72 (2007). Retrieved from http://cfha.info/journal72p11.pdf.

[216] On the other hand, Anglican leaders in Canada suspected all Quaker immigrants of being disloyal to the Crown. See Lise Hansen, "Friends and Peace: Quaker Pacifist Influence in Ontario to the Early Twentieth Century," Quakers Archives. https://quaker.ca/archives/document/friends-and-peace-quaker-pacifist-influence-in-ontario-to-the-early-twentieth-century/

[217] Fuller, "Parcel of Quakers."

use it to aid the militia."[218] Friends went to jail for refusing to pay the pacifist levy. Quakers who were eligible for militia service remained true to their Quaker principles, declined to pick up arms, and opted not to pay the required fine; instead they accepted the consequences. This was true of Friends both in the States and in Canada.

Although, Friends were not called to enlist for the Mexican-American War, they were asked to pay. Quakers refusal to pay the war taxes to support the war and their oppositions to the war, some believe, may have convinced President Polk to seek peace in 1848.[219] Friends, joined by Congregationalists and Unitarians, spoke often and strongly in opposition.

The American Civil War (1861-1865) did place demands on Friends to participate. Some Friends did enlist, having no other answer to the dilemma they faced from "the evils of slavery and war [doing] battle in their [Quaker] hearts and minds."[220] The dilemma was that

---

[218] Donald G. Anger, quoted in Jonathon Hodge, "The War of 1812 – Like all Wars – Was Not All Glory and Righteousness. Not Even Mostly Glory and Righteousness," Local History and Genealogy. Last Modified on May 22, 2012. https://torontopubliclibrary.typepad.com/local-history-genealogy/2012.

[219] April Pickens, "The Effect of Religious Opposition on the Mexican-American War (1846-1848)," *MAD-RUSH Undergraduate Research Conference* (April 10, 2015). https://pdfs.semanticscholar.org/7279/4c1a60c2832a024848a7feaf39b18cd5f48f.pdf.

[220] Robynne Rogers Healey, "Speaking from the Centre or the Margins? Conversations between Quaker and non-Quaker Historical Narratives," 2016 George Richardson Lecture, *Quaker Studies* 22, no. 1 (2017). https://online.liverpooluniversitypress.co.uk/doi/pdf/10.3828/quaker.2017.22.1.2.

John William Buys, in his 1973 doctoral thesis, sums up the dilemma nicely: "The coming of the war in1861, presented many Friends with a moral dilemma that produced continuing tension within the Society for the duration of the

of choosing "whether to prioritize the sanctity of union, support abolition, or remain neutral."[221] Enlisting caused many to be expelled from their monthly meetings and caused divisions within their families. But it was not just men, struggling whether to join the war, who had tough choices to make. In the words of Annika Jensen: "Quaker civilians also faced difficult choices; though she was a Southerner, Delphina Mendenhall welcomed starved and tattered Union soldiers into her home because it aligned with her religious principles of generosity and compassion."[222] Some Friends solved their dilemma whether to participate on either side, Confederate or Union, by moving as far from the battle scene as they could; going west to the territories. Some southern states, such as North Carolina, however, attempted to keep Quakers from leaving the state.[223]

The travelling Friends ministers, who carried the gospel well beyond their circles in the seventeenth century, may not have met with many others who were centered on the gospel like themselves. But, in the late eighteenth and early nineteenth centuries,

---

conflict. On the one hand, most Friends were loyal Republicans, sympathetic to Lincoln, and had a long history of opposition to slavery. On the other, they were traditionally opposed to war. Many Indiana Friends found it difficult to take a position against the war when they approved of the goals for which the war was fought." John William Buys. "Quakers in Indiana in the Nineteenth Century," (PhD diss., University of Florida, 1973). https://ufdc.ufl.edu/AA00022028/00001/1x

[221] Annika Jensen, "The Oatmeal Brigade: Quaker Life During the Civil War," The Gettysburg Compiler: On the Front Lines of History. Last Modified on December 18, 2015. https://gettysburgcompiler.org/2015/12/18/the-oatmeal-brigade-quaker-life-during-the-civil-war/

[222] Ibid.

[223] Doris McClean Bates, "The Quakers and Their War of Resistance," *Tar Heel Junior Historian* (Fall 2000). https://www.ncpedia.org/quakers-and-their-war-resistance.

after the progress of the Second Great Awakening and the growth of the Evangelical movement, these Friends began to encounter others who, although they did not come from the Friends tradition, knew the same Christ and were called to the same purpose. Elfrida Vipont suggests that this drew Friends from their isolation causing them to be "strengthened and refreshed by the fellowship of co-workers from other religious denominations."[224] As these new relationships increased, the Quietism began to diminish; Friends once again began to connect with the world around them. They shared with other evangelicals the need for a direct religious experience with acceptance of Christ as savior. They stressed the doctrine of Christ's atonement and began to put more emphasis on the Scriptures regarding them as the revelation of God. They began to promote education and Bible study and they revived their involvement in addressing the social issues of the day—alcoholism, prison abuse, immorality, unhealthy working conditions, and above all slavery.[225] Some Friends also addressed the spread of Deism and the concepts of Unitarianism and Universalism which were strong throughout these years.

Friends opposed the institution of slavery well before the American Civil War. In the nineteenth century, Friends continued the earlier efforts of John Woolman to abolish slavery and the slave trade. Friends, such as Benjamin Lundy, became abolitionists. Lundy organized the first abolition society in 1815, and, in 1821, he published the influential work, *The Genius of Universal Emancipation*. Quaker poet John Greenleaf Whittier joined Lundy in the publication of the *National Enquirer*, a publication devoted

---

[224] Vipont, 174.

[225] Bacon, 84-85.

to emancipation.[226] Sisters, Sarah and Angelina Grimke, left their family plantation in South Carolina in 1821 and moved to Philadelphia, where they joined with Friends.[227] They spent their life speaking and writing for abolition and also promoted women's rights.[228]

There were some Quakers who saw the need to use more than words in this struggle against slavery and who welcomed more active tactics. Beginning in 1819, in North Carolina, a system of safe routes and hiding places were created to assist slaves in their escape from slavery to freedom. This became known as the Underground Railroad. Levi Coffin, a Friend who had seen the evils of slavery in North Carolina, took on the role of president of the railroad.[229] Many Friends, including Isaac T. Hopper, Thomas Garrett, Laura Haviland, and Lucretia Mott acted as conductors and stationmasters, and many of these organized relief services for freed slaves following the war. Not all Friends were pleased with the underground activity, however, because it involved secrecy and falsehood.[230] In Indiana, in fact, because, in addition to working in the underground, Friends also housed fugitive slaves and joined abolitionist movements (which threatened older Friends traditions), the

---

[226] Errol Elliott, *Quakers on the American Frontier*, (Richmond: Friends United Press, 1969), 87-88.

[227] Sarah was convinced to become a member of the Friends by reading John Woolman's *Journal*.

[228] Barbour & Frost, 322-324. See also David Emory Shi, *America: A Narrative History*, 11th ed. (New York: W.W. Norton, 2019), 489.

[229] Elliot, 94. Perhaps it may be more accurate to state that he was ascribed that role by slave-catchers.

[230] Jesse Greenspan, "Eight Key Contributors to the Underground Railroad." Last Modified on February 9, 2019. https://www.history.com/news/8-key-contributors-to-the-underground-railroad

Yearly Meeting, 1842, divided into two yearly meetings, with one becoming the Anti-Slavery Yearly Meeting. The two divisions later reunited.[231]

William Penn had created penitentiaries in Pennsylvania which focused on rehabilitation rather than imprisonment. These penitentiaries became models for other colonies which, for a time, followed Penn's example of providing food, lodging, and work or training for prisoners. A society, the Pennsylvania Society for Alleviating the Miseries of the Public persons, was established in 1787 and promoted the "Pennsylvania System," which kept prisoners separated from each other. In the nineteenth century, Friend Thomas Eddy helped reform prisons in New York following the procedures promulgated by the society. Prison reform was also affected in England through the efforts of Elizabeth Fry. Elizabeth, who had come to join Friends through the preaching of William Savery and was opened to the needs in prisons by her friendship with Stephen Grellet in 1813, visited Newgate Prison in London and found conditions there deplorable. She brought these conditions to the attention of the public and personally visited the women in prison, establishing classes and means of employment for the imprisoned women. Inspired by Elizabeth, similar programs were created in Pennsylvania.[232]

Isaac Hopper, a Quaker heavily involved in the Underground Railroad and in various abolition activities, was a prison inspector who took his role seriously, personally visiting prisoners and working to provide for and to give guidance to released prisoners. He was an

---

[231] Eliott, 92-94.

[232] Bacon, 132-138.

agent of the Prison Association for New York City and helped establish associations in other cities and states. His daughter, Abby Hopper Gibbon, founded the first ever halfway house for women. Influenced by Hopper many monthly meetings established regular visitation programs and supported the Pennsylvania Society in their promotion of reform nationally.[233]

In the nineteenth century, the mentally ill were often displayed publicly for entertainment. Since Quakers believed in the indwelling of God within all humankind, this became a concern of Friends. They "believed that the mentally ill could be cured if treated with kindness and respect," and pushed for changes in the care of the mentally ill.[234] Isaac Hopper was also a major influence for changes in this area. He was joined by William Tuke, Thomas Scattergood, Thomas Eddy, and Thomas Kirkbride. William Tuke founded York Retreat in England and based treatment on Quaker principles of dignity and tenderness. Thomas Scattergood, who was a leader in education for children, established a similar institution in the States which was opened in 1813 as the Frankford Asylum outside of Philadelphia. Thomas Eddy likewise founded Bloomingdale Asylum in New York in 1818. Thomas Kirkbride established an association to assist others engaged in the same work.[235]

Abolition, prisons, care for the mentally ill were but three of the many concerns Friends addressed in the century. Joseph Lister, a

---

[233] Celia Caust-Ellenbogen, "Isaac T. Hopper," Quakers & Slavery. http://web.tricolib.brynmawr.edu/speccoll/quakersandslavery/commentary/people/hopper.php.

[234] Debbie Price, "For 175 Years: Treating Mentally Ill with Dignity," *New York Times* (April 17, 1988). https://www.nytimes.com/1988/04/17/us/for-175-years-treating-mentally-ill-with-dignity.html.

[235] Bacon, 140-142; Vipont, 163-164.

Quaker concerned for the general health and the high rate of deaths following surgery, created sterile atmospheres for surgery. The germ-killing product, Listerine, is named for him. His first sterile surgery was in 1865. With a concern for the alcoholism so prevalent in 1876, Charles E. Hires, a Quaker pharmacist invented the first soft drink, Root Beer, as an alternative for alcoholic beverages. Friends George and Richard Cadbury moved their chocolate factory out of the unhealthy conditions in Birmingham to rural Bourneville in 1879 because of their concern for the health and welfare of their factory workers. The new factory provided a number of amenities for workers. Joseph Rowntree concerned for the widespread poverty created decent and inexpensive housing. He also provided free education and a free library.[236] Other Quakers like Sir Titus Salt and William Lever concerned for people and society as well as business found ways to improve working conditions and the general well-being of workers.[237] Florence Kelley was an American Friend (1859-1932) who fought for workers' rights in the nineteenth century.[238] Although a Presbyterian, but greatly influenced by the Quakers, Sylvester Graham in the early 1800s concerned that school children in London were poor and undernourished created a cracker made from whole wheat and a sweetener which we know today as a Graham Cracker.[239] In 1841

---

[236] "Workers' Rights," Quakers in the World. http://www.quakersintheworld.org/quakers-in-action/169/-Workers-Rights.

[237] Richard Turnbull, *Quaker Capitalism: Lessons For Today* (Oxford: Centre for Enterprise, Markets and Ethics, 2014). http://theceme.org/wp-content/uploads/2015/07/Quaker-Capitalism.pdf.

[238] Barry Roche, "Florence Kelley: The Quaker Who Fought for the US Workers' Rights," *The Irish Times*. Last Modified July 19, 2017. https://www.irishtimes.com/news/ireland/irish-news/florence-kelley-the-quaker-who-fought-for-us-workers-rights-1.3159986.

[239] *Encyclopedia Britannica Online*, s.v. "Sylvester Graham."

two Quakers, Thomas Huntley and George Palmer, established a biscuit factory (Huntley and Palmers) where they "emphasized honesty, self-discipline, and hard work" and sold their products at a fair price. They provided a "sick fund and recreation facilities" for the families that worked for them.[240]

As Friends began, in the nineteenth century, to be drawn away from their isolation with the world some stayed close to Quietism, while others added to their Quietist personal devotion the evangelical thrust of the evangelical movement.[241] Travelling ministers began again to move beyond the boundaries of Friends. Friends with concerns for social reforms worked alongside other religious denominations.[242] Change to the Friends movement was bound to happen. Elders hoping to protect older traditions worked hard to keep Friends from having contact from the outside, but men such as Stephen Grellet and Joseph John Gurney brought an evangelistic fervor back into the movement.[243]

Grellet's evangelical message was bolstered by his understanding of the written word even as he was led and guided by the Spirit. But others had a quite different view. Elias Hicks, for instance, focused wholly on the light within, accepting no Scriptures or helps of any kind. Thus, Hicks discounted education, and training, or even preparation of a message, insisting only the revelation of Christ within one to be valid. Hicks dismissed the divinity and the atonement of Christ.[244] Those in the evangelical movement were

---

[240] The Huntley & Palmers Collection: Reading Biscuit Town. http://www.huntleyandpalmers.org.uk/.

[241] Vipont, 173.

[242] Ibid., 174.

[243] Ibid., 177-178.

[244] For a fuller presentation of the character and ministry of Elias Hicks see,

interested in promoting education and Bible study, and social action, and strongly preaching Christ Jesus as savior. Those who wanted to hold tighter to Quietism and the older traditions believed that quiet waiting and trusting the light within should be the sole authority for Truth. Since both sides of this conflict were articulate and strongly believed theirs was the essential Quaker message,[245] conflict was inevitable.

That conflict, the Great Divide, came in 1827 and 1828. As early as 1819 some meetings recognized the error of Hicks' understanding and in 1822 the elders of a meeting from Philadelphia attempted to meet with him but were not able to do so. In 1824 the Philadelphia Meeting for Suffering prepared a statement for the Yearly Meeting which was opposed by those who sympathized with Hicks but remained in the minutes. The statement affirmed the Friends belief in the authority of the Holy Scriptures and the divinity and sacrificial death of Jesus Christ.[246] Members of the Philadelphia Yearly meeting began to take sides.

It was at the 1827 session of the Philadelphia Yearly Meeting that Friends divided into two factions—one in favor of Elias Hicks and his message and one remaining loyal to the established Yearly Meeting. Under the leadership of John Comly those following Hicks determined to separate and moved to create their own meeting and did so after sending an epistle to all the meetings of the Philadelphia Yearly Meeting explaining their reasons for doing so.[247]

Williams, 170-174.

[245] Vipont, 178.

[246] Williams, 172.

[247] Ibid.

Walter Williams sums up the separation nicely:

> The die was cast. The process of separation had be-
> gun. Most of the local meetings had in membership
> some who sympathized with Hicks, and others who
> did not. The situation was charged with strong emo-
> tional elements. Meetings were torn asunder, fami-
> lies entertained separate loyalties; households were
> divided between the two groups. Tensions
> abounded, and bitterness found place in multiplied
> situations. Members of the country meetings in ma-
> jority aligned with the "Hicksites." In the cities the
> majority stood with the elders and Meeting for Suf-
> ferings of the original Society. [248]

Thus, Philadelphia Yearly Meeting was divided into two camps—
one being called Orthodox and the other called Hicksite. But the
division did not stop with Philadelphia. It spread throughout the
movement. New York Yearly Meeting split early in 1828, and
Baltimore later that year. Indiana Yearly Meeting remained with
the orthodox Friends although a number of Hicksite Friends left.[249]
Ohio Yearly Meeting also split in 1828 after a very undignified and
unruly Yearly Meeting session.[250]

The same forces that led to the increased interest in evangelism in
America were also at work in England. A new generation was
finding Quietism losing its appeal. Contact with other Christians
created the same new evangelical interests as in the States. A
number of traveling Friends from England, William Forster, Anna

---

[248] Ibid.

[249] Bacon, 88.

[250] Barbour, 178-179.

Braithwaite, Thomas Shillitoe, were in America speaking against heretical opinions and encouraging evangelism at the time of the Great Divide. Among the English preachers with strong evangelical leanings was the young Joseph John Gurney.

Joseph John Gurney, having completed his education and settled into a position in his father's bank, and while working with the British and Foreign Bible Society, determined to become a "Plain Friend," and gave much of his life speaking on behalf of the Society. In 1837, he traveled to America for a three-year mission "brought religious revival to many Quaker meetings which had been in a comatose condition, and reinstated an interest in education and Bible study, both of which had waned considerably during the long years of quietism."[251] Gurney was one who, as Elbert Russell said of him, "was evangelical in theology: Quaker in feeling, manner of life, and practice of worship. He put the Bible first as the authority for doctrine, but the Spirit first in the conduct of life and worship. "[252] Like George Fox, he "recognized the authority of the Holy Scriptures while at the same time [he] called men to heed the voice of the Spirit within."[253]

Both in England and in America, there were Friends feeling uncomfortable with Gurney's influence, since Gurney promoted Bible study in class groups, participated with non-Quakers in abolitionist activities, and worked with the British Bible Society. These activities could lead Friends away from the original Quaker message and dilute the solidarity of Friends. One of these concerned Friends was John Wilbur, from Rhode Island. For Wilbur

---

[251] Bacon, 89.

[252] Williams, 177.

[253] Ibid.

involvement in prison reform, Bible societies, and missionary work was "un-Friendly" and would destroy the distinctives of Friends. The "emphases, convictions, dress, speech, and procedures" of the founding Friends needed to be held to at all costs.[254]

John Wilbur met Joseph John Gurney as Wilbur toured England 1831-1833. There at a Yearly Meeting session in London he took Gurney aside to warn him of the dangers of his un-Friendly teachings. When Gurney came to the States in 1837 Wilbur followed after him attempting to convince those who had heard Gurney's teaching not to heed it.[255] The stage was set for an eventual separation. The separation came in 1845 when after New England Yearly Meeting attempted to silence Wilbur, he and those who sympathized with him withdrew to create their own New England Yearly Meeting of the Society of Friends, claiming to be the authentic New England Yearly Meeting.[256] Thus, the orthodox Friends were further divided into the Gurneyites and the Wilburites.

There were other conflicts that took place within the Friends in the nineteenth century. Early in the century Hannah Barnard, an American traveling in Ireland aggravated the tendency for rationalistic thinking in a small group led by Abraham Shackleton of Ballitore. Shackleton questioned several points of Quaker doctrine and questioned parts of the Bible. As clerk of Carlow Monthly Meeting he refused to read the queries because in them the word "holy" was applied to the Bible. Before this early incident was concluded Hannah Barnard was brought before the London Yearly

---

[254] Williams, 180-181. See also Barbour, 377.

[255] Williams, 180-183.

[256] Ibid., 183.

Meeting to question whether her teachings aligned with Friends or not. The Yearly Meeting pronounced against her and she was sent home to America. The Irish "New Lights" who were involved in the controversy were disowned.

Also in England at the same time as the Great Divide took place in America a small group of Friends felt led to expose the "errors of historic Quakerism" and published a book, *A Beacon to the Society of Friends,* written by Isaac Crewdon, clerk of Manchester Friends Meeting. Crewdon spoke against the notion of an inner light. He took exception to the teachings and emphasis that Friends placed on the Holy Spirit and pushed instead for the "utter supreme authority of Scripture." Most of those involved in the Beaconite movement left the Friends to join with the Plymouth Brethren.[257] One positive result of this controversy was that it forced the London Yearly Meeting to compose an official statement on the Holy Spirit.

In the last portion of the century the orthodox/evangelical Friends experienced revival, and out of the revival came several changes. Many meetings saw the need for pastoral leadership to keep the spiritual emphasis and Bible study moving forward.[258] The terminology of "the light within" or "inner light" began to be replaced with an emphasis on the person and work of the Holy Spirit.[259] As well, a move toward unity was begun.

In 1887 a conference was held in Richmond, Indiana, with representatives from ten American Yearly Meetings and from

---

[257] See Vipont, 182 and Williams 178.

[258] Cooper. *A Living Faith*, 7.

[259] Williams, 207-208. See also Ralph Beebe, *A Garden of the Lord: A History of Oregon Yearly Meeting of Friends Church* (Newberg: Barclay Press, 1968), 22.

London and Dublin. Out of this conference came a declaration of faith (The Richmond Declaration of Faith) which was a statement of the doctrines "held and taught" by evangelical Friends. Another conference in 1892 considered guidelines for pastoral systems. A third conference in 1897 established a unified discipline.[260] Unity instead of division was now the key word.

---

[260] Williams, 214.

Discussion Questions/Projects

1. If you were asked to characterize your local meeting or Yearly Meeting in one word what would that word be? Why would that word fit?

2. History texts use the term "revolutionary" in describing many aspects of the nineteenth century even though the great revolutions—1688, American, French—were from the centuries previous. What was revolutionary and why? How did this impact life in the nineteenth century?

3. Friends in America faced three different kinds of wars in the nineteenth century; one in which their country was invaded, one in which their country invaded another, and a civil war. How were the implications for Friends different in each of these? How might you have responded to any one of these?

4. With the travels of George Fox and the Valiant Sixty the Friends movement began with carrying the gospel outward to others. How and why did this change so that doing so was considered a departure from Friends customs?

5. What were the consequences of Friends reaching out to cooperate with those of the evangelical movement? What consequences are possible for Friends today participating in interdenominational projects?

6. Describe Deism, Unitarianism, and Universalism and contrast each with the beliefs of Friends in a comparative chart.

7. The text introduces only a handful of Friends who were involved in abolition campaigns. Do a broader study and compose a paper or a chart that gives a fuller picture of who and what was involved.

8. Laura Haviland and Levi Coffin had large bounties on their heads for their anti-slavery work. If you had been in their shoes, what would you have done?

9. Laura Haviland not only played a major role in the Underground Railroad but created educational opportunities for freed slaves. Research the Raisin Institute and prepare a short paper on her success.

10. Are Friends still actively involved in prison reform? How do criminal justice programs fit with the mission of the Friends Church?

11. Trace the effects of the Friends impact on the care of the mentally ill from the nineteenth century to the present. Who are the counterparts of Elizabeth Fry, Isaac Hopper, or William Tuke today?

12. Eighteenth-century Friends found great value in Quietism. Nineteenth-century Friends found value in evangelism. How can these two be blended together? What elements of each do you find most attractive?

13. Stephen Grellet had an interesting life story. With research compose a short biographical sketch.

14. Stephen Grellet obeyed God's call to preach in a wood in New Jersey. Not seeing anyone, nevertheless, he gave a full-length sermon on the love of God. Sometime later, he met a man in England, crossing the London Bridge, who stopped him and said that his life was transformed, and he became an evangelist after hearing Grellet's sermon in the woods, when Grellet thought he was speaking to no one. Have you had an experience or experiences of following the leading of the Holy Spirit, not knowing the reason for the leading, and finding out later the reason? If so, can you describe the experience? Is it essential that we discover the reason, or is it enough to be faithful to God, even though we may never know the reason?

15. Beginning with the Great Divide, compose a flowchart that details the separations leading to today's branches of the Friends movement. You will need to create a list of current Friends bodies to do this.

16. Consider the position of Elias Hicks. How do his beliefs and teachings line up with current Hicksite Friends? How do Hicks and current Hicksite Friends compare to today's evangelical Friends?

17. Compose a transcript for the dialogue that could happen if Joseph John Gurney, Elias Hicks, and John Wilbur were the guest panelists for a panel discussion on one of these topics: Three Essential Quaker Practices for all Friends, The Person and Role of the Holy Spirit, The Proper Place of Scripture in the Friends Meeting. Consider yourself as the moderator of the panel discussion.

18. Elisha Bates of Ohio was a contemporary of Elias Hicks. In 1825 he wrote a book detailing the "acknowledged" doctrines of Friends: *The Doctrines of Friends or Principles of the Christian Religion as Held by the Society of Friends*. (He uses "acknowledged" three times in his preface as if he were writing in contention of doctrines that were not acknowledged.) In the 1830s he supported those in the Beaconite movement who put extreme authority in the Bible. Locate a copy of Bates' book and examine his chapter on the Scriptures (Chapter VII). How does his view differ from Elias Hicks?

19. Could the Gurneyite/Wilburite separation have been avoided? Why or why not?

20. Look up a copy of the Richmond Declaration and compare the statement with what you understand primitive Quakerism accepted. Are there many differences?

For Further Study

Bacon, Margaret. *The Quiet Rebels: The Story of the Quakers in America.* New York: Basic Books, 1969.

Barbour, Hugh and J. William Frost. *The Quakers.* Richmond: Friends United Press, 1994.

Beebe, Ralph. *A Garden of the Lord: A History of Oregon Yearly Meeting of Friends Church.* Newberg: Barclay Press, 1968.

Cooper, Wilmer. *A Living Faith: An Historical and Comparative Study of Quaker Beliefs.* 2nd Ed. Richmond: Friends United Press, 2006.

Elliott, Errol. *Quakers on the American Frontier.* Richmond: Friends United Press, 1969.

Holden, David. *Friends Divided: Conflict and Division in the Society of Friends.* Richmond: Friends United Press, 1988.

Vipont, Elfrida. *The Story of Quakerism, 1652-1952.* Richmond: Friends United Press, 1977.

Williams, Walter. *The Rich Heritage of Quakerism.* 2nd Ed. Newberg: Barclay Press, 1987.

Laura Smith Haviland 1808-1898

Laura Smith was born into a Quaker family in Ontario, Canada.[261] Her father was a minister, and her mother an elder in the Friends Church. At age seven, her family moved to New York. She married Charles Haviland, and they moved to Raisin Township in Lenawee County, near Adrian, Michigan.

Influenced by the anti-slavery work of John Woolman, Laura and her friend, Elizabeth Chandler, operated the Raisin Anti-Slavery Society. The Havilands made their home a sanctuary for fugitive slaves, and it became part of the Underground Railroad. They established the Raisin Institute, a coeducational, integrated school, where many indigent children were educated. In their work they were threatened by gunfire. Further trouble came to Laura when her family contracted the skin disease, erysipelas, from which her parents, Charles, and one of her children died. She, too, was afflicted with the disease but recovered.

After her husband's death, Laura traveled to other states to aid slaves to freedom. On a train near Sylvania, Ohio, she was held at gunpoint. Afterward, slave hunters offered a $3000 reward for her death. The threats only increased Haviland's anti-slavery efforts in other states.

During the Civil War Laura added to her ministry by giving medical care to wounded soldiers and improving conditions for war prisoners being held in dehumanizing prisons. After the war she volunteered relief services for freed slaves, providing them with

---

[261] See Laura Smith Haviland, *A Woman's Life-Work: Labors and Experiences of Laura S. Haviland* (Cincinnati: Walden & Stowe, 1882).

food supplies, seeds for planting, and farm implements. She did extensive relief work in Kansas, and the town of Haviland, Kansas, the home of Barclay College, was named for her. Haviland, Ohio also bears her name. Other works of Haviland include her advocacy of women's rights and her leadership in the Great American Revival.

7
Friends in the 20th and 21st Centuries

1887 The Richmond Conference produces the Richmond Declaration of Faith.

1892 A second conference of Orthodox Friends considers the pastoral system.

1895 The Manchester Conference becomes a turning point for the Society in England.

1897 A third American conference prepares a Unified Discipline.

1900 Hicksite Friends join together in the Friends General Conference.

1902 The Five Years Meeting (which becomes the Friends United Meeting) is organized with all Yearly Meetings except Ohio and Philadelphia joining.

1926 Oregon Yearly Meeting (now Northwest) leaves the Five Years Meeting.

1926 Central Yearly Meeting is established (from members of Indiana and Western).

1937 Kansas Yearly Meeting (now Mid-America) withdraws from the Five Years Meeting.

1937 A second World Conference of Friends, Swarthmore Pennsylvania is held.

1937 The Friends World Committee for Consultation begins.

1952 A Friends World Conference is held at Oxford, England.

1957 Rocky Mountain Yearly Meeting is formed (from members of Nebraska).

1965 The Evangelical Friends Alliance (now Evangelical Friends Church International) is formed.

1966 The Five Years Meeting becomes Friends United Meeting.
1967 A Friends World Conference is held at Guilford College.
1970 A conference at Saint Louis gathers Friends from all persuasions.
2008 Evangelical Friends Church becomes Evangelical Friends Church International.
2014 First National Friends Multiplication Conference is held at Barclay College in Haviland, Kansas.

The twentieth century challenged Quakers with the same challenges as the eighteenth and nineteenth centuries. The Friends peace testimony was challenged by several wars. For English Friends it was, first of all, the Boer War; for all Quakers it was World Wars I and II, as well as the Cold War. American Friends also faced the challenge of the Spanish American War, the Korean War, and the Vietnam War.

Quaker beliefs were also challenged by the increasing influence of modern thought and the abandonment of religious sensibilities by the world's population. Further divisions also challenged Friends as small splinter groups separated from several of the Yearly Meetings and the union designed to join Friends together.[262] Other challenges were more positive. There were three challenges that began in the late nineteenth century that came into fruition during the twentieth and the twenty-first centuries. The first was the challenge to perfect a pastoral system among the orthodox Friends, while still retaining an identity as Friends. The second was the

---

[262] For example, Ohio Yearly Meeting and Philadelphia Yearly Meeting did not join the Five Years Meeting and later Oregon and Kansas Yearly Meetings disengaged from it. Members of Indiana, Western, and Nebraska Yearly Meetings left their respective meetings and formed new Yearly Meetings.

challenge of engaging in foreign missions. And third, there was the challenge of creating greater unity among all Friends.

Elfrida Vipont presents very clearly how the Boer War made the peace testimony a living issue for the new generation in England. Those who pled for "fair dealing and reason among nations" were bitterly opposed. Many Friends were accused of being "pro-Boer" and threatened with violence "because of their stand for moderation." Vipont records that "peace meetings were mobbed and howled down." Still, Friends did what they could "to expose and relieve the sufferings of the Boers in the concentration camps."[263]

In World War I, there were many young Friends who chose military service but not all. The American Friends Service Committee was organized in 1917 and arranged for alternative service for conscientious objectors. After the war, Friends were significantly involved in relief efforts that included Germans. Opportunities to bring relief to war-torn Europe were afforded through the American Relief Administration, led by Herbert Hoover, a Quaker. Opportunities for alternative service were much enlarged in World War II.[264] During the Second World War Friends helped in the relocation centers assisting children and others that were moved out of the bombed cities.

Friends attempted an initiative to thwart the Korean conflict before it began, and then moved into Korea, after the Korean War ended, to give relief and to rebuild. During the long Vietnam War, Friends took action by protesting peacefully against the war, by counseling

---

[263] Vipont, 244-245.

[264] Errol Elliott, *Quakers on the American Frontier* (Richmond: Friends United Press, 1969), 287.

and supporting conscientious objectors, and by providing humanitarian aid to both North and South Vietnam.[265] E. Raymond Wilson tells us that "more than one hundred Friends from nearly thirty states" aided the Friends Committee on National Legislation lobbying for peace during the Vietnam War. About 500 Friends attended the February Vigil for Peace in the early 1960s.[266] The Quaker United Nations Office, with centers in New York and Geneva was created to represent Friends concerns for worldwide peace and justice.[267]

The Second Great Awakening fostered revivals that continued throughout the nineteenth century. Evangelists such as Charles G. Finney, Dwight L. Moody, and Ira Sankey touched the lives of many men and women in America, England and the Continent. Quaker preachers Joseph John Gurney, William Forster, Stephen Grellet, Eli and Sybil Jones, Nathan and Esther Frame, and others encouraged revivals among Friends and kept revival active in local meetings.[268]

Bible classes and Sunday Schools increased in the nineteenth century among orthodox Friends with the efforts of Hannah Chapman Backhouse and Joseph John Gurney. The great number that were being added to the movement (because of the revivals)

---

[265] "Peace Witness and Relief Efforts during the Vietnam War," Quakers in the World. http://www.quakersintheworld.org/quakers-in-action/315/Peace-Witness-and-Relief-Efforts-during-the-Vietnam-War

[266] E. Raymond Wilson, Uphill for Peace; Quaker Impact on Congress (Richmond: Friends United Press, 1975), 293.

[267] Quaker United Nations Office. https://quno.org/

[268] Liberty Meeting (later Haviland) in Haviland, Kansas founded in 1885 became a Kansas revival center in the late 1880s and the first decades of the twentieth century. Nathan and Esther Frame were two of several evangelists in Haviland. See Glenn Leppert, "A Peculiar Meeting: The History of Haviland Friends Church," (Barclay College, 2011).

were longing for biblical education and discipleship. This, and the need to instruct these new members in the history and practice of Friends, led to calls for a change.[269] Meetings began to see the necessity of having someone available to organize and assist in preparing these new converts for membership and to provide instruction, encouragement, and counsel to the meeting as a whole. Meetings that adopted the pastoral system did so out of a sense of circumstantial necessity, rather than from internal conviction.[270]

Although Friends had hitherto resisted paid ministers, they had funded traveling ministers. With the need for pastoral help before them, they determined that they might have a travelling minister serve temporarily in one location.[271] These temporary assignments then became full time positions. Five years after the conference at Richmond another conference was held in 1892. One significant topic discussion at the conference was the subject of pastoral care. Papers and discussions at the conference looked at the need for such a pastoral system, as well as the dangers it might pose to the movement. The role of the pastor, training for the pastor, and the relationship between governance of the church and the pastoral role were each carefully weighed.[272]

---

[269] Barbour & Frost, *Quakers*, 211.

[270] Lorton Heusel, "The Quaker Pastorate," 1956 Quaker Lecture of Indiana Yearly Meeting, 1956, 3.

[271] Elliott, 124; Williams, 207-208. For a not so favorable view see Brinton, *Friends for 300 Years*, 194-195.

[272] *Proceedings of the Conference of Friends of America, held in Indianapolis, Indiana, 1892* (Richmond: Nicholson, 1892), 16.

The conference summed up their discussion with this minute:[273]

> This Conference desires to urge upon Friends every-where the importance of the diligent exercise of the various spiritual gifts bestowed by the Master, especially those of the ministry of the word and of the pastoral care of the flock of God. In connection with these services, the church is reminded of its duty in making such provision as may be necessary for the support of those who give their time to the work, so that the gospel may not be hindered, nor the shepherding of the flock impaired by the want of pecuniary means. At the same time that we strongly commend a proper pastoral system, we desire that Friends will be careful to see that it is not abused by the assumption of undue authority on the part of pastors, by their standing in the way of any service the Lord may lay upon others, or by leading members of the flock to look to, and depend upon human agency instead of the Divine Shepherd and Bishop of souls Himself. We believe that the faithful exercise of pastoral care is an important agency in the Master's hand in establishing and building up the membership of the church.

From this beginning, the pastoral system expanded and was firmly established by the early twentieth century. Three-fourths of the Society of Friends were pastoral by the beginning of the twentieth century.[274] This brought a major change to Quaker practice and

---

[273] Ibid.,

[274] Elliott, 253.

distinguished orthodox Friends from those of the General Conference.[275] Engaging pastors for a monthly meeting was uncharted territory, with dangers of giving too much control to pastors and losing the priesthood of believers as a core tenet. Both of these dangers were avoided. Many of the Yearly Meetings which adopted the pastoral system issued handbooks for pastors and meeting members. The system also engendered increased interest in education. Meetings created stronger educational programs and in order to have trained pastors, training programs were added to existing Friends colleges and the Kansas Central Bible Training School in Kansas was established in 1917.

Alongside a developing pastoral system, many of the orthodox Yearly Meetings also established mission programs. In fact, one of the main topics considered at the 1892 conference in addition to the pastoral system was "A Foreign Mission Board for all American Yearly Meetings."[276] While the creation of a board was approved in the twentieth century, mission boards to administer several mission fields were created by the individual Yearly Meetings (see chapter eight, "Friends and Missions.").

The greatest challenge of all was to bring unity back to the Quaker movement. The Great Divide had separated Friends into orthodox and Hicksite. The orthodox were further divided into Gurneyite and Wilburite factions. Further separations also occurred; for example, a small group left the Philadelphia Yearly Meeting calling themselves the "Primitive Friends" and a small group removed themselves from the London Yearly Meeting to become the

---

[275] Brinton, 194-196. See also Vipont, 223.

[276] *Proceedings of the Conference of Friends of America* (Richmond, Nicholson, 1892), 16.

"Fritchley Friends."[277]

Stirrings for unity began among Friends with the 1887 Richmond Conference and its counterpart in England, the Manchester Conference in 1895.[278] By 1900 Hicksite Friends were working together united by the Friends General Conference. The Yearly Meetings of the Gurneyite meetings after the Richmond Conference joined together to form the Five Years Meeting in 1902. This became the Friends United Meeting in 1966.[279] A "slow process of reunification of Hicksite and Orthodox [began] in the first half of the twentieth century."[280] In 1954 The Five Years Meeting represented the largest number of Friends in the world with thirteen Yearly Meetings as members and with many Friends groups sending delegates to the meetings.

Most of the integration of the wider body of Friends came through the auxiliary entities that came from Friends and from world conferences. Four world conferences were held beginning with a conference in London in 1920, then 1937 at Swarthmore College in Pennsylvania, 1953 at Oxford, and at Guilford College in 1967.[281] But the one thing that enabled the most cooperation was "the desperate need for joint service in the twentieth century."[282] The Friends Service Committee was established in 1915 by the London Yearly Meeting to deal with all matters of conscription and efforts

---

[277] Elliott, 73.

[278] The Manchester Conference became a turning point for English Friends as it refocused their attention to the Bible.

[279] Cooper, 7.

[280] John W. Oliver, Charles Cherry & Caroline Cherry, *Founded by Friends* (Lanham: Scarecrow Press, 2007), 63.

[281] Barbour, 341.

[282] Vipont, 232.

for peace. An American branch was established in 1917. The Friends World Committee for Consultation was established in 1937 at the World Conference at Swarthmore. It provided an organization for worldwide fellowship and cooperation. When the Five Years Meeting was set up in 1902 an American Board of Foreign Missions was also established to coordinate the mission efforts of the Yearly Meetings together. Although it did not bring unity between the Hicksite Friends and evangelical Friends the Evangelical Friends Alliance in 1965 (which became Evangelical Friends Church International in 2008) united evangelical Friends.

Today there are four bodies of Friends that, although they cooperate through the entities just mentioned, are four distinct bodies. There is the Friends General Conference comprising the Hicksite Friends. The Conservative Friends who maintain conservative methods including silent worship. Then there is the Friends United Meeting, the successor of the Five Years Meeting, with a large number of Yearly Meetings in its membership. Fourth, Evangelical Friends Church International is the joint effort of the evangelical Friends all around the world.

Friends United Meeting and Evangelical Friends Church International, both coming out of the Gurneyite tradition are quite similar. Friends in both affirm the ministry of all believers, most have pastoral meetings, emphasize the atonement of Christ, and strongly focus on the Great Commission with mission efforts around the world. Silent waiting, Bible Study, and prayer are also part of their worship. Conservative Friends also confirm the importance of loving Christ. Friends of the General Conference, often referred to as "liberal" Friends, hold strongly to the concept of the inner light being the foremost authority and practice silence in worship as did the early Quakers.[283]

The move for unity began in the nineteenth century and expanded through the twentieth century. The expansion of the organizations which allowed the Yearly Meetings to work together for vital concerns took place throughout the twentieth and into the twenty-first centuries mostly in America and England. It is interesting to note that the new entities and events happening in the twenty-first century worthy of listing on a timeline happened in East Africa and South America where the numbers of Friends exceeded that of North America and Europe.[284]

---

[283] Margery Post Abbott, Mary Ellen Chijioke, *et. al.*, *The A to Z of the Friends (Quakers)* (Lanham: Scarecrow Press, 2006), xxx.

[284] Margery Post Abbott, Mary Ellen Chijioke, Pink Dandelion & John William Oliver, *Historical Dictionary of Friends* (Quakers), 2nd ed. (Lanham: Scarecrow Press, 2012), xxiii.

Discussion Questions/Projects

1. Several challenges to the Friends movement are introduced in the opening paragraph of the chapter. What challenges do Friends face today that are not in this opening list? Catalog them and suggest why each is a challenge to our Quaker faith.

2. Research the beginnings of the Friends Service Committee (1915) in England and the American branch, the American Friends Service Committee (1917). Which unit earned the Nobel Peace Prize in 1947?

3. Quakers in Britain and America pushed initiated talks for peace before the Korean War began. See what you can find about the 1950 Friends Initiative of Peace in Korea which was a joint effort between the British East-West Relations Group and the American Friends Service Committee.

4. The text mentions a February Peace Vigil of the 1960s. Research the February Peace Vigil. When was it started? Is it still an active movement for peace?

5. We do not read about Friends being involved in the First Great Awakening but Friends were definitely part of the Second Great Awakening. Prepare a short paper on the Second Great Awakening examining the relation of this widespread revival with the revivals of the Friends.

6. Nathan and Esther Frame were Friends evangelists who were part of the revival center that formed in Haviland, Kansas in the 1890s. How was it that they left the Methodist Church to become Friends?

7. Joseph John Gurney was a member of the British and Foreign Bible Society and promoted Bible study everywhere he preached. Hannah Chapman (Gurney) Backhouse was his older sister. Research Hannah's travels and ministry as a Quaker teacher and promoter of Bible study.

8. Hannah Chapman (Gurney) Backhouse, Joseph John Gurney, Elizabeth (Gurney) Fry were the children of John and Jane Gurney. Create a biographical sketch of the family and account for the spiritual focus and commitment to ministry that these children exhibited.

9. Describe the connection between the great revivals that spread across the United States and the rise of the pastoral system begun among orthodox Friends. Why had Friends resisted such a system previous to this time?

10. Descriptions of the conference held at Richmond in 1887 and the program and discussions may be found in a number of sources. What happened at that conference that made it such a significant change-point for orthodox Friends?

11. Friends meetings are sometimes distinguished as either pastoral or non-pastoral. Some suggest instead that better terminology is programmed or non-programmed. What is the difference? May a pastoral meeting also be non-programmed? What about the distinction between church and meeting?

12. How did the Friends who adopted a pastoral system find their pastors? What areas were changed in this process?

13. Beginning with the Richmond Conference of 1887 there was a series of large conferences called to discuss matters pertinent to Friends doctrine and practice. The first of these, each held in the States, was followed by a set of conferences that involved Friends from all parts of the world. Compose a table that lists these conferences giving the name, the date, the location, and the concern that was prominent. Several of the texts listed in the "For Further Study" section will be useful for this task.

14. The text states that much of the cooperation of the Friends as a whole came through the entities created within Friends to focus on particular concerns. Make a list of those Friends organizations that are still functioning today and describe their area of concern and influence.

15. Rufus Jones wanted to bring unity among Quakers after the separations of the 19th century. One of his methods was to involve people of different beliefs into common service. What do you think of Jones' idea?

16. Although cooperation in areas of peace, or relief, or lobbying for Christian concerns have brought Friends together it has not mended the breach made by the Great Divide in 1827-1828. Do you believe this will happen or even should happen? Why or why not?

17 Elton Trueblood, a recognized Quaker author, advocated a reasoned, Christ-centered faith. Why do you think he wanted to combine reason and faith?

18. Outline your anticipation for the future of Friends and give reasons for your position.

For Further Study

Abbott, Margery Post, Mary Ellen Chijioke, et. al. *The A to Z of the Friends (Quakers).* Lanham: Scarecrow Press, 2006.

Abbott, Margery Post, Mary Ellen Chijioke, et. al. *Historical Dictionary of Friends* (Quakers). 2nd Ed. Lanham: Scarecrow Press, 2012.

Anderson, Paul. "Epilogue." In Walter Williams. *The Rich Heritage of Quakerism.* Newberg: Barclay Press, 1987.

Barbour, Hugh and J. William Frost. *The Quakers.* Richmond: Friends United Press, 1994.

Brinton, Howard. *Friends for 300 Years.* Wallingford: Pendle Hill Publications, 1972.

Brown, Derek. *On Quakers and Pastors.* Newberg: Barclay Press, 2019.

Cooper, Wilmer. *A Living Faith: An Historical and Comparative Study of Quaker Beliefs.* 2nd Ed. Richmond: Friends United

Press, 1990.

Elliott, Errol. *Quakers on the American Frontier*. Richmond: Friends United Press, 1969.

Heusel, Lorton. "The Quaker Pastorate." 1956 Quaker Lecture of Indiana Yearly Meeting, 1956.

Holden, David. *Friends Divided: Conflict and Division in the Society of Friends*. Richmond: Friends United Press, 1988.

Oliver, John. *Founded by Friends.* Lanham: Scarecrow Press, 2007.

Punshon, John. *Reasons for Hope: The Faith and Future of the Friends Church*. Richmond: Friends United Press, 2001.

Proceedings of the Conference of Friends of America, held in Indianapolis, Indiana, 1892. Richmond: Nicholson, 1892.

Vipont, Elfrida. *The Story of Quakerism; 1652-1952.* Richmond: Friends United Press, 1977.

Williams, Walter. *The Rich Heritage of Quakerism.* Newberg: Barclay Press, 1987.

Wilson, Raymond E. *Uphill for Peace; Quaker Impact on Congress.* Richmond: Friends United Press, 1975.

David Elton Trueblood 1900-1994

David Elton Trueblood was a prominent, eighth-generation Friends philosopher, theologian, and church leader. He was born in Pleasantville, Iowa in 1900 and died near Lansdale, Pennsylvania in 1994. He was known as "dean of American religious writers" and published thirty-seven books. Trueblood was educated at William Penn College (now William Penn University), Brown University, Hartford Theological Seminary, Harvard University, and Johns Hopkins Uni-versity, where he received his Ph.D.

Trueblood was interim chaplain at Harvard University, and he taught at Guilford College, Haverford College, Stanford University, where he was a tenured professor of philosophy and chaplain, Earlham College, and the Earlham School of Religion, which he helped establish as the first Friends seminary. He was editor of the Quaker periodical, *The Friend*, and was clerk of the Friends World Committee for Consultation. He was founder of the church renewal movement, Yokefellows International. Trueblood was advisor to the American presidents from Hoover to Reagan and served as Chief of the Religion Information Agency under the appointment of President Eisenhower. He presided at the memorial service of Herbert Hoover. He was also advisor to the Voice of America. Trueblood married Pauline Goodenow, with whom he had four children, and following her death, married Virginia Zuttermeister.

Elton Trueblood addressed such important topics as the disciplined life, the ministry of every Christian, and a reasoned, Christ-centered faith. During an interview in his ninetieth year, he identified himself as catholic (meaning non-sectarian); apostolic (being rooted in the New Testament faith); reformed (making changes when needed for improvement); and evangelical (i.e. Christ-centered). About his Christ-centered faith he said: "I speak everywhere

I go of the Christlikeness of God . . . I see Christ, not merely as the wise one, the good teacher, but my Savior and Redeemer." Trueblood is well known for his description of the Quaker faith. "Quakerism is the most Christ-centered religion. Other religions have liturgies and hierarchies. Quakerism has neither of these. If Quakers do not have Christ, they have nothing."

David Elton Trueblood, teacher, encourager, man of humor, mentor to writers, and friend to all who knew him, made a significant impact on the Friends movement in the twentieth century.

Norval Hadley 1928-

Norval Hadley sang tenor in a college quartet known as the Four Flats. That quartet was heard across the country in radio broadcasts and live performances. After college, beginning in 1956, Hadley, along with the other members of the quartet, traveled throughout Asia on behalf of the international relief agency, World Vision. "Billed as the World Vision Quartet, they sang at the U.S. Presidential Prayer Breakfast in Washington, D.C., in 1957 and 1960 and recorded four albums. The group disbanded in 1987."[285] Hadley continued to work with World Vision International, spending fifteen years in positions that led to service around the globe. For twenty-eight years, he was the prayer director.

In 1971, he became the General Superintendent of the Northwest Yearly Meeting of Friends.[286] He also served as the Executive Director of the Evangelical Friends Mission, overseeing mission work in eight nations. He was also a longtime member of the National Prayer Committee. In 1969-1970, he served with a peace negotiation team that went to Nigeria during the Biafran War.

While superintendent of Northwest Yearly Meeting, he founded a cooperative call for Christian peace, known as the New Call for Peacemaking. This cooperative joined the forces of the Mennonites, Church of the Brethren, and Friends.[287] Numerous conferences

---

[285] Nancy Haught, "Harlow Ankeny, Newberg, Part of the Four Flats Christian Quartet, Dies at 82," *The Oregonian.* Last Modified on January 10, 2019. https://www.oregonlive.com/living/2011/01/harlow_ankeny_newberg_part_o f.html

[286] "Norval Hadley," Notable Individuals, George Fox University Archives. https://digitalcommons.georgefox.edu/noteable_individuals/40/

[287] Margery Post Abbott, Mary Ellen Chijioke, *et. al., Historical Dictionary*, 159.

and published materials were produced.

Norval has written a number of books, most notably: *A New Call to Peacemaking* (1976), *Sin and the Sanctified* (1980), *Rwanda: In the Trail of the Red Horse* (1996), and *Encountering Jesus (2013* with David and Kim Butts).

Adrian Halverstadt 1960-

Adrian Halverstadt is chancellor, professor of criminal justice, and chair of the online Biblical Studies and Christian Leadership degrees at Barclay College. He teaches in both the undergraduate and the Master's studies. Earlier Adrian was appointed Academic Vice President at Barclay College.

Serving the wider Friends Church, Adrian is Leadership Facilitator of Rocky Mountain Yearly Meeting, Secretary of Evangelical Friends Church International, and Director of Evangelical Friends Church International-North America, which coordinates the ministry of all six Evangelical Friends Yearly Meetings in North America. Adrian was recorded as a Friends Minister in Evangelical Friends Church-Eastern Region, where he served as a Friends pastor for more than thirty years. He was Executive Pastor of Willoughby Hills Friends Church and a District Superintendent in Evangelical Friends Church-Eastern Region. While ministering in Eastern Region, he opened a mission field in Brazil. Further, Adrian served as Interim Pastor of the Pratt Friends Church (Evangelical Friends Church-Mid America Yearly Meeting). He continues to lead worship and preach in many Friends churches.

Adrian received the Bachelor of Arts degree from Ft. Wayne Bible College, the Master of Arts in Christian Ministry from Huntington University, and the Doctor of Philosophy (Ph.D.) degree in Theology, with a concentration in Conflict Management and System Theory, from Trinity/University of Liverpool. He also holds a graduate degree in Criminal Justice from American Public University.

Adrian is married to Lisa, and they are the loving parents of Adrian III, Joel, and Tim, and the proud grandparents of six precious and beautiful grandchildren. Adrian testifies that he loves the church and he is committed to biblical holiness. He says: "I am convinced that God can transform the world for His glory through Barclay College and the Evangelical Friends Church."

8
Friends and Missions

1654 George Fox records in his *Journal* "about sixty ministers had the Lord raised up, and now sent abroad out of the north country."

1658 Mary Fisher travels to see the Sultan of Turkey.

1671 George Fox makes a mission journey to North America.

1677 George Fox visits Holland and Germany.

1833 Daniel Wheeler visits the South Pacific.

1861 Joel and Hannah Bean spark interest among Friends by their ministry in the Sandwich Islands.

1868 The Provisional Committee on Foreign Gospel Service (1865) becomes the Friends Foreign Mission Association in Britain.

1869 Eli and Sybil Jones begin the mission school at Ramallah.

1871 Samuel Purdie arrives in Mexico.

1894 The American Friends Board of Foreign Missions is formed.

1902 A mission work is begun in East Africa.

1927 The Foreign Missionary Association and the Council of International Service join to become the Friends Service Council.

1978 Evangelical Friends Mission (EFM) is founded.

Several have noted: "the Quaker movement began with an explosion of missionary activity," that it was marked "by a stirring missionary spirit," and that "one of the outstanding characteristics of early Friends was a sense of mission."[288] Erroll T. Elliott remarks: "There was an urgent sense of mission that can hardly be doubted though the word and the plan of present-day missions were as yet unknown."[289]

As early as 1654 George Fox wrote in his *Journal*:

> About this time did the Lord move upon the spirits of many whom he had raised up, and sent forth to labour in His vineyard, to travel southward, and spread themselves in the service of the Gospel to the eastern, southern, and western parts of the nation, Francis Howgill and Edward Burrough to London; John Camm and John Audland to Bristol; Richard Hubberthorn and George Whitehead towards Norwich; Thomas Holmes into Wales; and many others different ways, for the Lord had raised up about sixty ministers, and did now send them abroad out of the north country.[290]

These sixty ministers, spreading themselves out across the country to share the gospel, were the first Friends missionaries.

Margaret Bacon reminds readers that, in the first quarter-century, individual Friends carried the gospel far and wide: Germany, Holland, along the Mediterranean, across the Atlantic to Barbados

---

[288] Bacon, 176; Vipont, 207; Williams, 51. See also Cooper, *Living Faith*, 16: "A strong missionary spirit caused early Friends to proclaim the Gospel message and to call people to repentance."

[289] Elliott, 295.

[290] Fox, *Autobiography*, 83. Note that the *Journal of George Fox*, a revised edition by John Nickalls, refers to seventy rather than to sixty (p. 174).

and the new colonies in North America.[291] While the Valiant Sixty carried the good news to all parts of England, Thomas Holmes and his wife, along with Alice Birkett, shared the gospel in Wales in 1654. William Edmonson carried the message to Ireland and Christopher Fell, George Wilson, and John Grave ministered to a receptive Scotland.[292]

"With a vision for the whole world"[293] to know Christ, other Friends scattered themselves farther than the British Isles. Before the end of 1655, Mary Fisher and Ann Austin took the gospel to the West Indies. Later, they moved on up to Boston, where they were immediately placed in jail. Mary Fisher, in 1658, traveled all the way to Turkey to present the gospel to the Sultan of that great empire. George Fox, along with a number of others, made a missionary journey to the Caribbean and the North American colonies during the period of 1671-1673.[294]

Engaging in missions seemed the unquestioned thing to do among those early seventeenth-century Friends. D. Elton Trueblood explains: "If a man [was] reached by Christ directly, in his own heart there was no alternative to an explosive response which involved the effort to bring other people to a similar experience of newness of life. Consequently, each man had to find some way of engaging

---

[291] Bacon, 176.

[292] Williams, 58-59.

[293] Gene Pickard, "An Evaluation and Revision of the Missions Program at Friends Bible College," (D.Miss. Diss., Trinity Evangelical Divinity School, 1986), 4.

[294] Williams, 61. For a delightful telling of the story of Mary Fisher's visit with Mahomet IV, the Sultan of Turkey in 1658 see Chapter 28: "Silver Slippers: or a Quakeress Among the Turks," in L. V. Hodgkin. A Book of Quaker Saints.

in missionary activity."[295] Seemingly possessing an understanding of Fox's vision of a great people to be gathered, early Friends were ready to live out the charge that George Fox gave them:

> Let all nations hear the word by sound or writing. Spare no place, spare not tongue or pen, but be obedient to the Lord God and go through the world and be valiant for the Truth upon earth . . . And this is the word of the Lord to you all, and a charge to you all in the presence of the Living God. Be patterns, be examples in all countries, places, islands, nations, wherever you come, that your carriage and life may preach among all sorts of people, and to them.[296]

It may be noted that, as John Punshon states: "The early Quakers had been totally committed to mission. They sought to convert the Jew, the Pope, the Sublime Porte, Prester John, the Emperor of China and everybody else."[297]

The seventeenth-century missionary zeal was greatly diminished as Friends moved from the seventeenth to the eighteenth century. When the persecution dimmed, so also did the initial enthusiasm of the movement, along with the spontaneous vitality of the missionary spirit. As Friends moved into the period of Quietism, their focus receded from the world around them to the world among them. Quiet waiting, deep pondering of the things of the Spirit, and a great concern to keep in place the early traditions were substituted for the spreading of the gospel message far and wide.

---

[295] Trueblood, *People Called Quakers*, 248-249.

[296] Quoted in Elton Trueblood, 249. From Fox, *Journal*, Nickalls, 263.

[297] Punshon, 215.

The leaders in the time of Quietism mentioned in Chapter 5—
Anthony Benezet, Thomas Chalkley, Rebeca Jones, Catherine
Phillips, David Ferris, William Savery, and John Woolman—were
concerned for spiritual growth and service, but they mostly
ministered to Friends and not to those outside of the movement.
Visits, like that of John Woolman to the Native Americans, were not
characteristic. In the eighteenth century, at the time of the Great
Divide among Friends, when Friends became split into Hicksite and
orthodox camps missions was one of the points of contention.
Some were fearful that mission work would emphasize human
efforts and not the leading of the Holy Spirit; that the organization
needed to do missions would result in a pastoral system.[298] Doing
missions would have called them to give thought to or to plan out
religious projects and the concern that missionaries would need to
serve as hirelings would contradict the longstanding tradition of no
paid ministry.[299] Their concern for the inward experience and the
maintenance of tradition left them without the inclination to reach
outward.

That inclination was awakened, in the late eighteenth century,
under the influence of the evangelical awakenings with John and
Charles Wesley and George Whitefield.[300] It became more intense
with the evangelical awakenings in the nineteenth century. But it
grew slowly; proposals for entering into mission work were
considered and rejected several times in London Yearly Meeting
from 1821 to 1830 and in America, the concept was also slow to be

---

[298] Trueblood, 252.

[299] Punshon, 216. See also Cooper, 169.

[300] Pickard, 24. See also Cooper, 169.

accepted.[301]

With no organized support for mission work, individuals began on their own to visit and to minister in areas where the gospel had not been taken. In 1833 Daniel Wheeler visited the South Pacific. In 1861 Joel and Hannah Bean sparked interest among Friends by their ministry in the Sandwich Islands. In 1869 Eli and Sybil Jones began the mission school at Ramallah. In 1871 Samuel Purdie arrived in Mexico.[302]

A turning point happened in 1860 when George Richardson, who had gone to Norway in 1858, wrote the first of 60 some letters to *The Friend* (a monthly journal published in London) urging Friends to consider how much more effective it would be with organized mission efforts rather than "brief and transient visits by individuals."[303] Richardson died before any action was taken, but Henry Stanley Newman took up the concern and in 1865 convinced London Yearly Meeting to establish a Provisional Committee on Foreign Gospel Service which began with support for new work in India and in Madagascar.[304] In 1868 the Provisional Committee became the Friends Foreign Mission Association. By 1920 it coordinated the work of some 120 missionaries in "Bhopal, India, Ceylon, Pemba, Syria, and Madagascar."[305]

In America, an American Friends Board of Foreign Missions was organized as an independent body in 1894. In 1902 this board was

---

[301] Pickard, 24.

[302] For a more comprehensive list, see Cooper, 170.

[303] Cooper, 170. See also Pickard, 26.

[304] Pickard, 27.

[305] Cooper, 171. See also Pickard, 27.

incorporated into the newly created Five Years Meeting. By 1912 this board was coordinating the mission endeavors of seven Yearly Meetings who had turned their fields over to it. The seven were Kansas (now Mid-America), Indiana, Western, Oregon (now Northwest), New York, Wilmington, and North Carolina. In 1918 New England Yearly Meeting turned their work over to the board as well.[306]

When Oregon and Kansas Yearly Meetings disengaged from the Five Years Meeting in 1926 and 1937, they established their own mission fields. Oregon began work in Latin America in Bolivia. Quakers began work in Africa in Rwanda, Burundi, and Kenya. Paul Anderson wrote in the "Epilogue" to *The Rich Heritage of Quakerism*:

> Friends in East Africa have quite an influence. Jack Kirk has suggested that some parts of East Africa may be considered 'Quaker' in much the same way that parts of Latin America could be considered 'Catholic'.[307]

In 1978, Evangelical Friends Mission (EFM) was established. Since then, some of the mission fields which were pioneered by Northwest Yearly (NWYM), Evangelical Friends Church - Mid America Yearly Meeting (EFC-MAYM), Evangelical Friends Church Southwest (EFCSW), and Evangelical Friends Church - Eastern Region (EFC-ER), were subsumed under EFM, which now has missions in Africa, Asia, Europe, South America, Latin America, Philippines, and Haiti. Several Yearly Meetings independently

---

[306] Elliott, 296.

[307] Paul Anderson, "Epilogue" in Walter Williams. *The Rich Heritage of Quakerism* (Newberg: Barclay Press, 1987), 282-283.

oversee mission work in various nations and in North America.

The Five Years Meeting became Friends United Meeting (FUM) in 1966. Coordinated today under FUM are mission fields "scattered from the Caribbean to Palestine, Africa to North America, and scattered places in between."[308]

There are no specific mission fields listed at the Friends General Conference (FGC) website, but FGC offers programs that provide relational tools and ways to combat racism. Likewise, there are no mission fields listed for Conservative Friends. The Yearly Meetings within the Conservative Friends work "to help spread the message that Christ has come to teach His people Himself. Through this labor [they] welcome seekers, finders, and returning strayed sheep to the worship of God in Spirit and in Truth."[309]

---

[308] Friends United Meeting, "Where We Work," https://www.friendsunitedmeeting.org/where-we-work/where-we-work.

[309] "Welcome to Our Meeting," Conservative Friend, https://www.conservativefriend.org/.

Discussion Questions/Projects

1. The Valiant Sixty spread out across England two by two carrying the gospel and the great news that Jesus could teach his people himself. Obtain a copy of *The Journal of George Fox* with a good index or find a copy online and follow the entries for the members of this group mentioned in the quotation from Fox's *Journal*.

2. If you have a copy of Fox's *Journal* with a good index read through the index and discover how many countries are mentioned in the *Journal*. Who ministered in each of these?

3. A significant meeting was held in 1660 at Skipton in Northern England which is known as the Skipton General Meeting. An important letter came from this meeting and was sent to "the Brethren of the North." With research see if you can identify the three authors of the letter and what the letter meant for the Friends missionary efforts in the seventeenth century.

4. This quotation from John Punshon mentions a number of significant leaders who were sought out by Friends: "The early Quakers had been totally committed to mission. They sought to convert the Jew, the Pope, the Sublime Porte, Prester John, the Emperor of China and everybody else." See if you can discover who these were and what Friends shared the gospel with them.

5. Suppose that you could have been present at a debate between a Hicksite Friend and a Gurneyite Friend on the value of missions. Write out a short dialog that might have occurred between them.

6. Research the evangelical awakenings with John and Charles Wesley and George Whitefield and present your findings in a short paper.

7. Individuals who went on their own to do mission work before the organized mission boards were created include Hannah Kilham, James Blackhouse, Daniel Wheeler, Isaac Sharp, William Forster, Eli and Sybil Jones, George Richardson, Robert Metcalfe, and Joseph Sewell. Prepare a short biography of any two of these making sure to describe the field they chose.

8. Like the men and women mentioned in #7 above God often places desires in our hearts. Where do you desire to be in mission for God - at home or in another nation? Why?

9. See what you can find about the activities of the Friends Service Council today.

10. Prepare a short paper describing the activities of today's Evangelical Friends Mission (EFM).

11. The website for the Friends United Meeting describes the mission activities as "scattered from the Caribbean to Palestine, Africa to North America, and scattered places in between." See if you can find specifics.

For Further Study

Anderson, Paul. "Epilogue." In Walter Williams. *The Rich Heritage of Quakerism*. Newberg: Barclay Press, 1987.

Cooper, Wilmer. *A Living Faith: An Historical and Comparative Study of Quaker Beliefs*. Richmond: Friends United Press, 2006.

Cattell, Everett. *Christian Mission: A Matter of Life*. Richmond: Friends United Press, 1981.

Elliott, Errol T. *Quakers on the American Frontier*. Richmond: Friends United Press, 1969.

Hodgkin, L. V. *A Book of Quaker Saints*. London: Longmans, 1968.

Pickard, Gene. "An Evaluation and Revision of the Missions Program at Friends Bible College," D.Miss. diss.,Trinity Evangelical Divinity School, 1986.

Punshon, John. *Portrait in Grey: A Short History of the Quakers*. 2nd ed. Fitchburg: Quaker Books, 2006.

Stansell, Ron. *Missions by the Spirit: Learning from Quaker Examples*. Newberg: Barclay Press, 2009.

Thomas, Nancy. *A Long Walk, a Gradual Ascent: The Story of Bolivian Friends Church in its Context of Conflict.* Eugene: Wipf and Stock, 2019.

Trueblood, D. Elton. *The People Called Quakers: An Enduring Influence of a Way of Life and a Way of Thought.* Richmond: Friends United Press, 1966.

Willard and Doris Ferguson

Willard and Doris Ferguson were Evangelical Friends missionaries in Burundi and Rwanda from 1962 until 2002. Willard's interest in missions began when, as a member of a Friends Bible College brass and vocal trio called the King's Kords he traveled to Haiti for a short-term mission trip. There, Willard felt a call to serve as a missionary. From an early age, Doris had intended to be a missionary nurse. She and Willard married in 1959, and moved to Hays, Kansas where Willard completed a Bachelor's and Master's Degree in Biology.

They served in Burundi for twenty-three years (1962-1985) where Willard taught first at a teacher training school established by the Friends Church and later at a Bible school maintained by a consortium of evangelical missions. Doris served as a nurse at the Friends Mission hospital. They also spent four years as dorm parents at a school for missionary children.

In 1986, the Fergusons were asked to go with George and Dorothy Thomas, long-time Friends missionaries in Burundi, to Rwanda with Evangelical Friends Mission, to establish the Friends Church in Rwanda. Starting from scratch was very challenging and also very rewarding. Willard's goal was to develop a leadership cohort within the Rwandan community to lead the church. A happy day was turning over the Legal Representative responsibilities to a talented Rwandan pastor.

Willard loved interacting with students and loved teaching. Among his favorite subjects were Creation Science and the Doctrine of Holiness. In Burundi he taught secondary school students, and in Rwanda he taught pastors. Both in Burundi and Rwanda he served as Legal Representative for the mission, and the church.

Burundi and Rwanda are unfortunately well-known for the paroxysms of ethnic violence that have swept these respective countries. Willard and Doris were present in Burundi in 1972 and the tense aftermath of genocide there and were evacuated from Rwanda during the Rwandan Genocide of 1994; returning as soon as they could to help rebuild the Friends Church and aid in the reconciliation efforts in the aftermath of this historic bloodletting.

The Fergusons served in Rwanda until September 2002 and spent six months teaching in Burundi in 2004. After spending a year as chaplains for senior living residents at Link Care in Fresno, CA, they retired to Haviland, Kansas where Willard had the opportunity to again teach his favorite subjects, science and Doctrine of Holiness.

One of his students wrote this about Willard: "We have all known of his and Doris Ferguson's Christ-filled work amidst the persecution and genocide in Rwanda. But I have the privilege to share how blessed I was to have this godly man as a professor for Doctrine of Holiness . . . The class had its challenges, but this class was far more challenging in personal and spiritual ways. It was the best class I had at Barclay. And who better to teach sanctification than Willard, a pure- hearted man. [I was] very blessed to have known Willard while at Barclay."

Brad and Chelsea Carpenter and Children

Brad and Chelsea Carpenter are graduates of Barclay College (2005 & 2007) who have been on the mission field in Rwanda since 2006. They have three children: Sarai, Gideon, and Ian.

Brad and Chelsea work with and support the leaders of EFC-R (Evangelical Friends Church-Rwanda). Their primary focus is D for D (Discipling for Development), which is a whole-life discipleship ministry. D for D emphasizes the lordship of Jesus in every aspect of life: spiritual, physical, and relational. The Carpenters have witnessed amazing and deep transformations in individuals and communities, and they are asking the Lord to spread this disciple-making movement throughout Rwanda and beyond. Brad works with Rwandan colleagues in visiting communities, preparing lessons, and coaching Rwandans in the D for D ministry. Brad participates in vision-casting and assisting EFC-R to become a mission-sending church. Chelsea spends much of her time serving her family and the missionary team. The Carpenter children (Sarai, Gideon, and Ian) are growing, learning, and enjoying the beautiful "country of a thousand hills." [310]

---

[310] "The Carpenter Family," EFM Rwanda,
https://catalog.friendsmission.com/campaign/efm-rwanda-or-the-carpenter-family/c202269

9
Friends Beliefs, Testimonies, and Practices

Beliefs

Beliefs are those truths that Friends put their trust, faith, confidence in unquestioningly. Evangelical Friends beliefs are drawn from the Scriptures. Hicksite and Conservative Friends beliefs are drawn from their emphasis on the "inner light" or "that of God in everyone."

Testimonies and Values

Testimonies are the core values that Friends testify to or hold as important elements of their faith. Testimonies would include: simplicity, peace, integrity, community, equality, and stewardship.

Practices

Practices are standard ways that Friends organize their life and worship, and how they behave in their world. Coming to the sense of the meeting in making decisions, waiting quietly in worship for the Lord to speak, these are practices.

As mentioned in the earlier chapters of this book, there is a difference, regarding beliefs, between Evangelical Friends and Conservative Friends. Friends believe that Christ is in the world to enlighten everyone (John 1:9) and refer to this belief as the "inner light" or "that of God in everyone." But, at the second division of Friends when Friends were split into two camps, the Conservative and the Gurneyite, the divisive question was whether this inner light alone was sufficient, or if revelations from God (as in the Scriptures) could and should also be part of the Friends beliefs. Conservative Friends held to the sufficiency of the inner light while

Evangelical Friends also believed enlightenment came from the Scriptures. While Friends had traditionally declared that they were non-creedal or had no established creed or doctrines, Evangelical Friends began to compose statements of faith and to commit their beliefs to writing not as creeds, but rather as explanations for understanding and defense of Truth.[311]

A creed is an authoritative formula of belief, or a statement that regulates what someone of a particular persuasion may believe. Early Friends, and some Friends today, firmly believe that there is no creed or formal set of beliefs that one must hold to be a Quaker. This is true because they believe that everyone can experience God within themselves. Evangelical Friends, on the other hand, although they do not have creeds, do have statements of belief. These statements are descriptions of what Friends believe, do, and encourage.[312]

A careful reading of *The Journal of George Fox* indicates that Fox did not shy away from making doctrinal statements (or statements of belief). He described the work and person of Jesus Christ. He declared the role of the Holy Spirit. He described Christ's teaching on prayer. He made a clear presentation of salvation. He detailed the need for and the way of righteousness. Many other doctrinal concepts are also found especially in his *Journal*. In addition, Fox wrote a number of books. In 1674, he recorded:

> During the time of my imprisonment in Worcester. I
> wrote several books for the press, one whereof was

---

[311] Howard Brinton, *Guide to Quaker Practice* (Wallingford: Pendle Hill, 1942), 7. Brinton writes: "Friends have never officially issued statements of their beliefs comparable in authority to the creeds of many other Christian bodies." He explains this is because of the inadequacy of words to express a living faith.

[312] Jack Willcuts, *Why Friends are Friends* (Newberg: Barclay Press, 1984), 41.

called "A warning to the English;" another was "To the Jews, proving by the prophets that the Messiah is come;" another, "Concerning inspiration, revelation, and prophecy;" another, "Against all vain disputes;" another, "For all bishops and ministers to try themselves by the Scriptures;" another, "To such as say, we love none but ourselves;" another, entitled, "Our testimony concerning Christ;" and another little book concerning "Swearing," being the first of those two given to the Parliament. Besides these, I wrote many papers and epistles to Friends, to encourage and strengthen them in their services for God, which some endeavoured to discourage them from; especially in their diligent and watchful care for the well-ordering and managing of the affairs of the church of Christ.[313]

In 1671, George Fox wrote a letter, to the governor of Barbados, that stressed the foundation upon which all Friends beliefs were grounded:

And we own and believe in Jesus Christ, His (God's) beloved and only begotten Son, in whom He is well pleased; who was conceived by the Holy Ghost, and born of the Virgin Mary; in whom we have redemption through His blood, even the forgiveness of sins; who is the express image of the invisible God. We believe that He was made a sacrifice for sin, who knew no sin; that He was buried, and rose again the third day by the power of His Father, for

---

[313] Fox, *Autobiography*, 331-332.

our justification; and that He ascended up into heaven, and now sitteth at the right hand of God. This Jesus, who was the foundation of the holy prophets and apostles, is our foundation. There is no other foundation.[314]

George Fox was not alone in writing pamphlets and books to explain and defend the Friends understanding. By 1662, according to Hugh Barbour and J. William Frost, there were several who had written systematic presentations of Quaker beliefs.[315] Robert Barclay, who became a Quaker in 1666 and accompanied Fox on numerous journeys, addressed many complaints and questions directed toward Friends in several small books and in his major work, his *Theses Theologica*, known as the *Apology* (the full title: *An Apology for the True Christian Divinity: Being an Explanation and Vindication of the Principles and Doctrines of the People Called Quakers*). In the *Apology*, he wanted to establish Quaker thinking within the context of the Friends faith. He did this by detailing fifteen propositions that summarized the concepts of the Friends.[316]

After 1845, numerous others wrote explanations, or defenses, of Friends beliefs, especially for Friends in the evangelical division. The *Richmond Declaration* of 1887 was "a statement of doctrines held and taught"[317] by Friends.[318] Elias Bates, in 1868, published

---

[314] Arthur Roberts. *The People Called Quakers*. (Newberg: Oregon Yearly Meeting of Friends Churches Board of Publications, n.d.), 10.

[315] Barbour & Frost, 63.

[316] Glenn Leppert, "Robert Barclay and Barclay College," paper presented at Barclay College, Haviland, KS, 1990, 2.

[317] Williams, 214.

[318] A copy of the Richmond Declaration may be found as Appendix C in Walter

The Doctrine of Friends or Principles of the Christian Religion as Held by the Society of Friends Commonly Called Quakers.[319] About the same time, John Bevans published a smaller volume, *A Brief View of the Doctrines of the Christian Religion as Professed by the Society of Friends.*[320] Centuries later, in 1970, Paul Barnett wrote, *Why I am A Quaker* to "help preserve and understand Friends teachings."[321] And in 1984, Jack L. Willcuts wrote *Why Friends are Friends* describing "some core Quaker convictions."[322]

Friends beliefs are central Christian beliefs and are rooted in Scripture.

God—Friends believe that God is the only one God. "Hear, O Israel: the Lord our God, the Lord is one" (Mark 12:29).

God is the transcendent, eternal, sovereign Creator. "In the beginning God created the heavens and the earth" (Genesis 1:1).

Yet God is immanent and personal; to whom we can pray and with whom we have personal relationship. Jesus called God, Father, - an intimate name. "Our Father in heaven" (Matthew 6:9).

God is all loving and loves the whole world. "For God so loved the world that he gave his one and only Son, that whoever believes in him shall not perish but have eternal life" (John 3:16).

Williams, *Rich Heritage of Quakerism.*

[319] Elias Bates, *The Doctrine of Friends or Principles of the Christian Religion as Held by the Society of Friends Commonly Called Quakers.* Printed by the author, 1868.

[320] John Bevans, *A Brief View of the Doctrines of the Christian Religion as Professed by the Society of Friends* (Philadelphia: The Friends Bookstore, nd.).

[321] Paul Barnett, *Why I am A Quaker* (Printed by the author, 1970).

[322] Willcuts, *Why Friends are Friends.*

Jesus Christ—Jesus Christ is the Incarnation of God. He was fully human and fully God. God was most fully revealed in Christ. God was in Christ fully, ultimately, supremely, perfectly.

Christ is eternal and was with God in the beginning. "In the beginning was the Word, and the Word was with God, and the Word was God" (John 1:1).

Yet Christ was fully human and shared human experiences and feelings. "Jesus wept" (John 11:35). He suffered death on a cross.

Christ is Lord – the one to whom we give ultimate loyalty and allegiance. George Fox and Robert Barclay often referred to Christ as Lord.

Christ is Teacher. Friends frequently call Christ Inward Teacher. In John 13:13, Jesus spoke of himself as Teacher and Lord. "You call me Teacher and Lord, and rightly so, for that is what I am."

Christ is Savior, who heals, forgives, and transforms us. In Luke 19:10 Jesus stated his mission: "For the Son of Man came to seek and to save the lost." His salvation was made possible by his sacrificial death and victorious resurrection.

Christ is ever-present. He assured us that "where two or three gather in my name, there am I with them" (Matthew 18:20).

Christ is our Light. John 1:9 tells us: "The true light that gives light to everyone was coming into the world."

Jesus is our friend. He explained in John 15:14: "You are my friends if you do what I command."

Holy Spirit—In his farewell address to his disciples, Jesus told them: "But the Advocate, the Holy Spirit, whom the Father will send in my name, will teach you all things and will remind you of everything I have said to you" (John 14:26). Historically Friends have emphasized the truth of the Holy Spirit, whom we can experience firsthand for enlightenment, guidance, and inspiration.

Trinity—Quakers believe in the Trinity: God, Christ, the Holy Spirit – three eternal persons in one. Our belief in the Trinity affirms the unity of God – God is one, the divinity of Father, Son, and Holy Spirit, the paradox of three in one – God is three, yet one. Although "early Friends questioned the metaphysical speculation in some creedal expressions . . . they affirmed the creative, redemptive, and empowering work of the Father, Son, and Holy Spirit."[323]

Human Nature—Humans are created in the image of God. "So God created mankind in his own image, in the image of God he created

---

[323] Paul Anderson, personal correspondence with David Kingrey, 5-22-2020. Paul stated: "On early Friends objecting to creedalism (trinity, etc.), liberal Friends have often misunderstood the bases for those objections, just saying "Quakers are non-creedal, so there's liberty to believe anything you want ...". A more accurate analysis would go something like this; Early Friends objected to leveraged ways that creedal confessions were used to mark insiders and outsiders within authentic Christianity for three overall reasons: (a) the primary factor in Christian vitality is intimate acquaintance with God (the spiritual relationship) rather than knowledge about God (abstract content); (b) following the example of Jesus, early Friends also opposed legalistic adherence to the laws of God, prioritizing covenantal faithfulness to the ways of God; (c) early Friends held primarily to the clear teachings of Scripture, as inspired by the Holy Spirit, over and against their dogmatic interpretations by religious authorities.

In these ways, Friends were seeking to be faithful to the author of Scripture, the Holy Spirit, working through human agencies across the bounds of time and space. And, every Yearly Meeting has its own Faith and Practice, describing its understandings of these issues, to which its membership is expected to adhere."

them" (Genesis 1:27). "God saw all that he had made, and it was very good" (Genesis 1:31).

Every person has the light of Christ within. "The true light that gives light to everyone was coming into the world" (John 1:9).

The Holy Spirit is within us. Jesus explained to his disciples: "But you know him [the Holy Spirit], for he lives with you and will be in you" (John 14:17).

Friends believe in the goodness of human life, created in God's image, and in whom the Holy Spirit lives and the inward light of Christ illumines. This faith in the intrinsic worth of every person is at the heart of the Quaker social testimonies of integrity, non-violence, and equality. Such a positive view of human life is grounded in the redemptive power of Jesus Christ. However, we "all have sinned and fall short of the glory of God" (Romans 3:23) and are in need of Divine forgiveness.

Church—The Church is the universal fellowship of Christians commissioned to take the gospel to the whole world. The Great Commission of our Lord is to "go and make disciples of all nations" (Matthew 28:19).

The individual fellowships are called churches or meetings.

Bible—Quakers believe that the Bible is the inspired written word of God. Friends also believe that the same Spirit who inspired the writers of Scripture inspires us directly. So we test our personal leadings of the Holy Spirit with Scripture and interpret Scripture as we are led by the Spirit of God. George Fox frequently wrote in his *Journal* that the Spirit who gave forth the Scriptures will lead us into truth. The Bible is the written word of God. Christ is the Living word.

Eternal Life—Friends believe in the eternal fellowship promised by Jesus: "For God so loved the world that he gave his one and only Son, that whoever believes in him shall not perish but have eternal life" (John 3:16).

Friends Testimonies and Values

Testimonies—Testimonies are the core values (or virtues) that Friends testify to or hold as important elements of their faith. Wilmer Cooper defines testimonies in this fashion: "an outward expression of an inward leading of the Spirit," or "faith incarnated into action."[324] Testimonies are "deeply rooted" in Friends religious faith and experience.[325]

There are many admonishments to live these testimonies in Fox's *Journal* and in the early writings and letters of Friends. Friends placed emphasis on living with high moral standards, integrity, spiritual strength, and courage. For example, notice this list of admonitions from George Fox:

> . . . live the life of the scriptures; live and walk in the Spirit of God; do not live in the life and power of those false; walk and live in and follow after Truth so that in light, in life, in love you may live; live and walk soberly in the Truth of Christ; live in the Lord's power and life; therefore live in the power of the Lord God; live in the pure wisdom, counsel, and instruction from God; live in the power of God; live

---

[324] Cooper, 128. See also https://quno.org/quaker-values.

[325] Cooper, 128.

in peace, in Christ, the way of peace, and therein
seek the peace of all men and no man's hurt; Live a
peaceable and godly life in all godliness and
honesty. So dear Friends, live all in the peaceable
Truth and in the love of it, serving the Lord in
newness of life. [326]

As Friends engaged in the mission of declaring Truth to their age
they came to be known as people of simplicity, honesty, and
faithfulness especially to each other. Common core values or
virtues soon became associated with Friends. Kim Hays in her
study, *Practicing Virtues*, gives four central virtues that were
commonly seen as Friends testimonies: equality, community,
simplicity, and peace[327] and contends:

Equality, community, simplicity, and peace are all
chapters in the Quaker story of fostering the Inner
Light in every individual. In a peaceful environment
where people feel equal to one another, share a
strong sense of community, and live simply and
single-mindedly, it is easier for that of God, or what
is best in every individual, to emerge.[328]

Others expand the list of Friends testimonies to include six core
virtues: simplicity, peace, integrity, community, equality, and
stewardship.[329] Additionally, kindness, honesty, and service are

---

[326] Fox, *Journal*, Nickalls, 160, 162.

[327] Hays, Kim. *Practicing Virtues: Moral Traditions at Quaker and Military Boarding Schools* (Berkeley: University of California Press, 1994).

[328] Ibid., 80.

[329] "S-P-I-C-E-S: The Quaker Testimonies," *Friends Journal*. Last Modified September 10, 2010. https://www.friendsjournal.org/s-p-i-c-e-s-quaker-

testimonies listed by still others.

David Kingrey, in the preface to this book, listed eight values: simplicity, integrity, equality, peace, education, missions, community, and stewardship. These may be considered in couplets: simplicity and integrity, equality and peace, education and mission, community and stewardship.

Both **simplicity** and **integrity** are, as Richard Foster says of simplicity: "an inward reality that results in an outward life-style."[330] "From the earliest days of the Quaker movement Friends were concerned about simplicity and honesty," says Leonard S. Kenworthy and he shares two reasons for this. First, they lived in a time characterized by "excesses, sham, and superficiality." Living simply was a way to counter this culture. Secondly, they realized that if they were to have time to commune with God and to interact with their world their lives would need to be simplified. In addition, in order to devote what they had—time, energy, resources—to Christ, they needed to live lives that were not complex and complicated.[331]

To those early Friends living simply meant dressing without ornamentation, dwelling in simple sturdy but not ostentatious homes, keeping their recreation uncomplicated, and not going overboard for events such as weddings and funerals.[332] Simplicity was a way to keep their priorities straight. If their priority was sharing Christ with their neighbors or taking the Truth to nearby

---

testimonies/.

[330] Richard Foster, *Celebration of Discipline: The Path to Spiritual Growth* (San Francisco: Harper San Francisco, 1998), 79.

[331] Kenworthy, *Quakerism*, 115.

[332] Ibid.

areas then they would not take on business or responsibilities that would prevent them from doing that. For Friends today, simplicity might mean living with self-discipline that removes the overburdened schedules that many attempt to keep setting aside things that detract and that upset our priorities.[333]

The familiar use of the term Quaker or a symbol of a Quaker to indicate integrity is well known. The symbol is valid because early Friends considered honesty and forthrightness to be highly important. They took literally the biblical injunctions "swear not at all" and "let your yea be yea and your nay be nay." Their word was as good as their bond and they lived by their word.[334] They would go to jail for not taking an oath believing there was no reason to swear an oath if they lived truthfully all the time; there was but one standard not one for daily life and another for the court. The American Friends Service Committee has stated correctly: "For Friends, having integrity means being authentic and having consistency between one's values and one's actions."[335] A simple way to sum up integrity is this: "living as whole people who act on what [they] believe, tell the truth and do what [they] say [they] will do."[336]

The two testimonies, **equality** and **peace**, focus on how Friends value others. Early Friends believed in equality. They believed women had rights and gifts that enabled them to participate in ministry. They were concerned for equal rights for Native

---

[333] Cooper, 134.

[334] Kenworthy, 116.

[335] "Integrity: Consistency in Word and Deed," American Friends Service Committee. https://www.afsc.org/testimonies/integrity.

[336] "Quakerism," Philadelphia Yearly Meeting of the Religious Society of Friends. https://www.pym.org/introducing-pym-quakers/quaker-testimonies/.

Americans. They had the same concern for the mentally ill, for prisoners, and for the poor. They were the first to outlaw the slave trade and to set their slaves free. In their view all were equal and were to be treated equally; thus, they would not honor one person over another by doffing a hat or using titles. They stressed equality to the point even of not using the plural "you" to address an individual. Friends believe that everyone, being created in the image of God and having "that of God in each," has worth and should be treated with dignity.[337]

A Quaker query on peace is simple: "How can I nurture the seeds of peace within myself, my community, and the world?" The concept of peace is three-fold. It entails the absence of conflict within one's self; a tranquility of the spirit. Second, it is an absence of conflict in the community whether that is a family, a town, a country, or the world. Third, peace is a sense of order and security.[338] The testimony of peace for Friends involves all three. Integrity requires inner peace. Equality involves seeking absence of conflict and living in order and security is a basic Friends pursuit. Peace for Friends is both a testimony and a practice. (*The practice of peace is covered later in this chapter.*)

The Friends testimony on peace is perhaps best exemplified by Hebrews 12:14: "Make every effort to live in peace with everyone and to be holy; without holiness no one will see the Lord." Peace must be pursued; it is not a natural outcome. Hafsat Ariola of Nigeria states this well: "Peace comes from being able to contribute the best we have, and all that we are, toward creating a world that supports everyone."[339] Living in peace is the outcome of

---

[337] Cooper, 138-139.

[338] Ibid., 137-138.

[339] "Peace: Peace Making at the Home and Abroad," American Friends Service

living simply and living with integrity and accounts for the Friends concern for equality.

The Quaker peace testimony is rooted in the teaching of Jesus in Matthew 5:9: "Blessed are the peacemakers, for they will be called children of God." In his book, *Following Jesus: The Heart of Faith and Practice*, Quaker scholar Paul Anderson wrote a chapter entitled, "Blessed Are the Peacemakers." In it he said:

> Jesus' counterviolent teachings on peace are entirely clear. He calls his followers to love others – including their enemies – to renounce violence and return good for evil, to embrace the way of his kingdom rather than resorting to force, to serve others rather than seeking to dominate them, to put away the sword, to forgive and not to avenge, and to embrace the cross – even if faithfulness exacts a price. In calling for alternatives to violence, Jesus offers a peace that is not of this world, and he blesses the peacemakers of every generation.[340]

Values—Friends have had a longstanding concern for both **education** and **mission**. Both are strongly held values for Friends. For them, the meeting house and the schoolhouse were side by side and in fact, often in the same building.[341] The first concern for nearly every new Friends settlement after establishing a place to worship was a school. Schools were begun as early as 1668 for the

---

Committee. https://www.afsc.org/testimonies/peace

[340] Paul Anderson, *Following Jesus: The Heart of Faith and Practice* (Newberg: Barclay Press, 2013), 159-160.

[341] Williams, 229; Rufus Jones, *The Faith and Practice of the Quakers* (Richmond: Friends United Press, n.d.), 144.

"honest and useful" instruction of children both "relating to divine principles" and to what might be needful for "the outward creation."[342] George Fox himself encouraged Friends to create schools so that the students ". . . by frequent reading of the Holy Scripture and other good books, that being seasoned with the truth, sanctified to God and taught our holy, self-denying way, they may be instrumental to the glory of God and the generations."[343]

At first, Friends maintained schools for Quaker children, and for the most part this was a "guarded education," meaning that it was designed to cover things useful for members of the Friends movement. But the concept of education was expanded as Friends moved into the late eighteenth and early nineteenth centuries. Friends pioneered boarding schools and often the Quaker schools gave rise to early efforts for public education. Friends stressed Bible study and many were involved in First Day School (Sunday Schools) [344] and in the Adult school movement.[345] Several Quaker schools begun in the 1830s later became the first Quaker colleges. Between 1856 and 1917 fifteen Friends Colleges were founded in America.[346]

The Friends concern for missions, that is, concern for completing the Great Commission, has already been considered in a previous chapter. But mission in the sense of purpose is also a Friends testimony. Each Friend has a purpose, a reason for being, a call of God upon their life. Members of the Evangelical Friends Church

---

[342] Williams, 229.

[343] Jones, *Faith and Practice*, 143.

[344] Ibid., 152.

[345] Vipont, 152-153.

[346] John Oliver, et. al, xii-xv.

International give their purpose as: "[meeting] the spiritual needs of their communities."[347] Those of the Friends United Meeting claim "by the power of the Holy Spirit to gather people into fellowships where Jesus Christ is known, loved, and obeyed as Teacher and Lord."[348] The stated vision of the Friends General Conference is to provide "loving service and witness in this world."[349] Conservative Friends continue the original mission of the early Quakers: "to help spread the message that Christ has come to teach His people Himself."[350] The mission has not changed since the time of the movement's founding. George Fox had a vision of a "Great crowd of people to be gathered" and he invited others to join him in that gathering. As they did so they declared with boldness that Jesus was come to teach his people himself. The same mission characterizes Friends today. Friends continue to gather people to Jesus and to meet the spiritual needs of their communities.

Two additional values are important to Friends—**community** and **stewardship**. From the very beginning, Friends worked together. The Valiant Sixty went, two-by-two, across England. Friends on mission went in small groups. Socially, they settled in communities where there was much interaction among them: Newberg, Oregon; Haviland, Kansas; Richmond, Indiana; Philadelphia, Pennsylvania;

---

[347] "About the Evangelical Friends Church," Malone University, https://www.malone.edu/about/affiliations-memberships/about-the-evangelical-friends-church/.

[348] Friends United Meeting. https://www.friendsunitedmeeting.org/.

[349] FGC: Friends General Conference. https://www.fgcquaker.org/about/vision-statement.

[350] "Welcome to Our Meeting," Conservative Friend. https://www.conservativefriend.org/.

one may trace the movement of Friends across the United States by the communities they settled. But community was much more than just clustered physical dwellings and the daily interactions that the geography engendered. Community entailed the joining of hearts and minds together in their "gathered meetings," where fellowship and worship blended together; there true corporate worship could be experienced. This sense of being "gathered" gave rise to responsibility and accountability with one another.[351]

The Friends understanding of "that of God in everyone" meant that one may encounter God directly and places the responsibility of connecting with God on the individual. Yet, finding God and connecting with truth brings the individual into the community. This is important for Friends in a number of ways. Meeting for worship with a mind for business, the calling of clearness committees to ascertain the best approaches and coming to the sense of the meeting are all Friends practices that depend on and deepen the sense of community.[352]

Stewardship (valuing and caring for all of God's creation) is a tenet of Friends. Virginia Schurman notes that George Fox often quoted Psalm 24:1: "The earth is the Lord's and everything in it, the world, and all who live in it," as he reminded folks that the world belonged to God. Friends believed (and still do) "that everything was created to be in harmony and right order with God and with each other."[353] A current statement on one Friends website is typical: "To Friends, good stewardship means taking care of what has been given, not

---

[351] Cooper, 199.

[352] "Community," About Quakers. http://about.bym-rsf.net/community/

[353] Virginia Schurman, "A Quaker Theology of the Stewardship of Creation," *Quaker Religious Thought* 74, no. 6 (1990). Retrieved from https://digitalcommons.georgefox.edu/qrt/vol74/iss1/6.

just for ourselves, but for the people around us and for future generations as well."[354] From another we read: "[God] made [humankind] the stewards of what was and remains God's by creation and rulership. We, therefore, are permitted the use of the earth and its resources, but as stewards must use them wisely, carefully, and as under the eye of their owner."[355]

Friends Practices

Practices are where the beliefs and the testimonies of Friends are lived out; where what one believes and testifies to as most important are put into daily practice. The following practices will be considered: the Friends practice of baptism and communion, the way Friends make decisions and seek the sense of the meeting, the Friends position on guidance, not taking oaths, peace and peacemaking, their use of queries, and how Friends worship.

Friends practice both **baptism** and **communion**. Friends "believe positively and profoundly in Baptism and in Communion. But they are such real and effectual experiences that [they] cannot be lowered to the level of rites or ceremonies."[356]

Friend Paul Anderson states: "Friends believe that baptism is the only hope to living under the lordship of Jesus Christ."[357] John the Baptist stated: "I baptize you with water. But one who is more

---

[354] "Stewardship Testimony," Fort Myers Quakers: Religious Society of Friends. http://fortmyersquakers.org/about-quakers/stewardship-testimony/.

[355] EFC-MAYM, *Faith and Practice: Part One*, 19. Retrieved from https://efcmaym.org/wp-content/uploads/2012/01/FP-PART-I.pdf.

[356] Rufus Jones, "Baptism and Communion," (American Friend Publishing Company, n.d.), 1.

[357] Paul Anderson, "Friends and the Sacraments," (Newberg: Department of Christian Testimonies, Northwest Yearly Meeting of Friends Church, n.d.).

powerful than I will come . . . He will baptize you with the Holy Spirit and fire" (Luke 3:16). In the words of Charles S. Ball: "Friends believe that baptism with the Holy Spirit is fully commanded and essential for salvation."[358] Friends do not practice water baptism, for water baptism was a sign of a changed life used by John the Baptist as he prepared the way for the coming of Christ. With Christ came a new possibility—the baptism or total submission into Christ and the radical change that becoming one with Christ brings.

The term baptism, meaning to immerse, is used four different ways in the New Testament: 1. Baptism with water as a sign of change and commitment; 2. Baptism with the Holy Spirit as in Matthew 3:11, filling the believer with the Holy Spirit; 3. Baptism into suffering as in Mark 10:38-39 in which the believer shares in Christ's suffering; and 4. Baptism into the teachings or into the leadership of another as in I Corinthians 10:2.[359] Friends see that Christ did not baptize (John 4:2). They note that Paul baptized only a few. But all believers filled with the Holy Spirit who have died and risen with Christ are baptized with the Holy Spirit and are in Christ. This is the true baptism that Friends practice. The word of Christ in the Great Commission: "Therefore go and make disciples of all nations, baptizing them in the name of the Father and of the Son and of the Holy Spirit, and teaching them to obey everything I have commanded you" is the fourth use of baptism mentioned above, that is, a baptism into the lordship of Christ.

---

[358] Charles Ball, *Remembering Our Heritage: Studies in Friends Beliefs* (Whittier: California Yearly Meeting, 1973), 19.

[359] Charles Beals, *The Essential Baptism* (Newberg, Barclay Press, n.d.), 3-4. See also Charles Ball, 17-18 and Herman Macy, *What About the Ordinances?* (Newberg: Barclay Press, 1965), 15.

Water baptism is an outward ordinance and, although a significant and meaningful symbol of commitment, it is not essential. The essential baptism is inward. Water baptism is a picture (or foreshadowing) of what are now spiritual realities in Christ. We no longer need the "figures, types, and shadows"[360] since we are able now to be baptized in Christ.

Friends also practice **communion** or the celebration of the Lord's Supper, but they do not require physical elements to do so. Friends interpret the observance of the "Lord's Supper" spiritually rather than literally. The Lord's Supper was enacted that evening before the crucifixion as a memorial to carry the disciples through the time that Jesus would be absent from them. But with the coming of the Holy Spirit, Christ was no longer absent. He was back and residing in their hearts. No memorial is needed when the presence of the Lord is real.[361] Communion for Friends involves sharing with Christ, participating with him and having an "intimate spiritual relationship"[362] with the Lord. Charles Ball says it well: "Thus spiritual and true communion depends upon the receiving of the Lord Jesus Christ and the presence of His Spirit in the believer's heart and life." It is an act of love and faith that does not depend on ritual or symbol.[363]

Decision making among Friends is a practice that distinguishes Friends from other Christian denominations. Friends do not vote. Friends do not seek consensus, nor do they make decisions based on the majority position. Rather, Friends believe and practice

---

[360] Beals, 11.

[361] Macy, 36.

[362] Ball, 24.

[363] Ibid.

gathering a sense of the meeting and allowing that sense of the meeting to become the decision. They seek to discover a sense of God's desires, rather than their own, in the decisions to be made. Thus, it may take time and much prayer for a decision to be made.

Decision making is part of waiting and worship.[364] The process begins in a meeting for worship where business may be conducted. It begins with silent waiting before the Lord and then out of that silence come voices sharing received truth. The process is different than consensus or majority rule because, as Arthur M. Larabee points out, the basic question is different. Whereas consensus asks, "What can we agree to?" and majority rule asks, "How do we vote?" gathering the sense of the meeting asks, "How are we led?"[365] The waiting, the worshiping, the listening, is because the decision must be attuned to the Spirit's leading.

Finding the sense of the meeting does not always end in perfect agreement. There may be some among those in the meeting who may not accept fully the truth revealed to others. This process allows for these to "stand aside." They may make clear to the group that "although they may not agree with the decision, they are willing to trust the corporate judgment of the meeting." This allows them, with a free conscience, not to hold up the decision making process.[366]

Closely related to the process of decision making is the Friends understanding of **guidance**. The first great opening that George Fox

---

[364] Barbour, 110; Cooper, 107-108.

[365] Susan Nagel, "Understanding Quaker Decision-Making," Friends School of Minnesota Blog. Last Modified on August 30, 2012. https://blog.fsmn.org/2012/08/understanding-quaker-decision-making/

[366] Cooper, 108.

had was when he heard the words: "O! then I heard a voice that said, 'There is one, even Christ Jesus, that can speak to thy condition'" and he understood "that Christ had come to teach his people Himself."[367] Fox found that it was Christ "who enlightens, and gives grace, and faith, and power." He testified:

> [It was by Christ's] power, light, grace, and Spirit, I should overcome also, I had confidence in Him; so He it was that opened to me when I was shut up and had no hope nor faith. Christ, who had enlightened me, gave me His light to believe in; He gave me hope, which He Himself revealed in me, and He gave me His Spirit and grace, which I found sufficient in the deeps and in weakness. [368]

From Fox's encounter in 1648 with a priest at Nottingham when he declared that it was the Holy Spirit that gave the Scriptures and who would lead God's children, Friends have put great emphasis on the leading of the Spirit. Silent worship, waiting, praying, heeding the Spirit-given "inward light of Christ within them" became their principle means of guidance. It is still true today. Friends practice silence so that they may be Spirit led.

From the very beginning, as mentioned in an earlier section on integrity, Friends had a single standard. There was no truth for daily living that was not also the truth for business and civic affairs. Friends believed Christ's words in Matthew 5, "Swear not an oath at all . . . all you need to say is 'Yes' or 'No'; anything beyond this comes from the evil one" (Matthew 5:34-37). There was no reason

---

[367] Fox, *Autobiography*, Jones. Retrieved from https://ccel.org/ccel/fox_g/autobio/autobio.vi.html.

[368] Ibid.

for Friends to take an oath because their daily lives were lived in truth and their words no matter the occasion were a truthful yes or no. Friends refused to take oaths and many of them suffered in prison for this. George Fox and other early Friends repeatedly reminded governmental officials that no oath was necessary for one who habitually spoke the truth. He urged that Friends be allowed simply to affirm or to declare that they would only speak the truth.[369] In 1696 the Affirmation Act in England allowed English Friends to affirm rather than take an oath. The act is still followed today by British and American Quakers.

Quaker author Howard Macy, in his book, *The Shalom of God*, has written about the significance of the Friends **peace testimony** in our world today: "The world hungers for peace. People have more than an appetite for peace; they are starved for peace . . . Quakers have shared this hunger and have acted for peace from their first generation."[370] Friends do more than talk of peace or refuse to go to war. They are actively assuring that young Friends men and women can declare a position as conscientious objectors and not have to take a military role in war. They have created many peace initiatives both to prevent and to end wars. They teach peace and peacemaking. In the world today are a number of Friends organizations which promote peacemaking including: the American Friends Service Committee (AFSC), the Center on Conscience and War, the Friends Committee on National Legislation (FCNL), Friends Peace Teams (FPT), a National Campaign for a Peace Tax Fund, and the Quaker House.[371]

---

[369] Williams, 75.

[370] Howard Macy, *The Shalom of God* (Newberg: Barclay Press, 2018), 7.

[371] "Alphabetical Listing of a Variety of Friends Organizations, Philadelphia Yearly Meeting of the Religious Society of Friends. https://www.pym.org/faith-

Friends use **queries** as a means of self-reflection. As early as the 1680s Friends began to use queries or a series of questions which were read regularly in meeting to cause reflection.[372] One current Friends group defines their queries as:

> . . . questions that guide personal and group reflection on how our lives and actions are shaped by Love and Truth. The emphasis is on how to live a life more completely aligned with the life of the spirit. Quakers often find Queries a powerful spiritual discipline. Returning again and again to the same prompt for deep reflection can set the stage for new understandings, changes of heart, and a rising sense of loving action that needs to be taken. If you can answer a Query with a "yes" or "no," try to grapple a bit more adding "why," "how," and "when" to the original query.[373]

Here are several simple queries: Are you open to the many ways the Spirit may speak to you? What does love require of you? Do you maintain an appropriate balance among work, service, worship, family, and recreation? Are you ready to rest if God asks it of you? Is every aspect of your life open to the transforming power of God? What stands in the way?[374]

---

and-practice/friends-and-some-of-their-organizations/alphabetical-listing-variety-friends-organizations/.

[372] Barbour, 109.

[373] "A Word about Quaker Queries," FGC: Friends General Conference. https://www.fgcquaker.org/sites/default/files/attachments/A%20Word%20about%20Quaker%20Queries_0.pdf.

[374] Ibid.

The heart of the faith of Friends is **worship**. Responding to the light that enlightens everyone, that is, to Christ, worship is the adoring response of the heart and mind to the influence of the Spirit of God.[375] Worship is not relegated to a certain time or place. It needs no elements, no rituals, and no forms. Instead it is waiting on, listening to, communing with the Spirit—worship must be in spirit and in truth.

D. Elton Trueblood, in describing worship among early Friends, says: "They simply gathered, listened, waited, and sought to be obedient."[376] These meaningful verbs describe still how Friends worship. Although an individual can worship at any time anywhere, Friends do gather together joining hearts and minds into one body. More correctly it might be said not that they gather together but that they are gathered together; the passive voice being more correct as it is the Spirit that draws them to the light. Gathered they open themselves to hear the whispers of the Spirit as they wait for God's word for each of them and for them as a body. Above all, they "center down" in the presence of God because they seek to be obedient.

Most Conservative Friends as well as Friends of the General Conference today gather, listen, and wait in silence. Sometimes it is a full deep silence, with no one called to share a message. At other times, there may be several who are led to speak. Evangelical Friends also center down in silence to listen and, out of the silence, there may be some who are led to share. Yet these Friends also add

---

[375] *The Richmond Declaration of Faith* (Richmond: Friends Publication Board, 1922).

[376] Trueblood, *People Called Quakers*, 88.

to the waiting Scripture reading and the singing of praise songs and hymns. Most Evangelical Friends also include a sermon or expository lesson as part of their worship. The one constant, whether it is conservative or evangelical bodies, is the quickness to accept and follow the Holy Spirit's leading among those gathered. No Friends meeting for worship is rigid in following an order of service; the Spirit may lead them to silence, to a multitude of shared messages, or perhaps to an intense time of vocal prayer.

Discussion Questions/Projects

1. Knowing what one believes is an important component of one's faith. Have you pondered the beliefs you are convinced of or do you take for granted whatever truths characterize your faith family? Are you able to write out without research a statement of faith of your own?

2. Prepare two arguments that might be used in a friendly debate among Friends. One argument would be that the inner light, which is Christ enlightening everyone, is sufficient for spiritual guidance and understanding and that no other doctrines or beliefs are necessary. The second argument is that in addition to the inner light it is important to have the Scriptures and statements that help us understand them.

3. Compose a definition of a creed and give examples of historic creeds used in the Church universal. What creeds can you find that are used in churches today? How does a creed differ from a statement of faith?

4. If you have access to a copy of *The Journal of George Fox* that has a good index, compile the statements Fox makes concerning the great doctrines of the faith such as salvation, or grace, or faith.

5. From the college library catalog, or from gleaning books on Quaker history, compose a bibliography of Quaker writings that focus on doctrine.

6. What biblical evidence do you find for the Quaker belief in the goodness of human life? (see Humanity in the statement of faith above). How do you see this belief relating to the Friends peace testimony and their testimony against capital punishment?

7. The Friends belief in ministry (under Christian Work in the statement of faith above) is that every Christian is a minister and has a ministry. How is your vocation a ministry? Or, how will your possible future vocation be a ministry?

8. Testimonies are the core values that Friends testify to or hold as important elements of their faith. What are your core values? Have you had occasion to testify of the importance of these values for yourself? Were you able to do so?

9. Which of the Quaker testimony/testimonies has the most meaning to you? Why?

10. In what ways can the Quaker testimony on simplicity be practiced today?

11. Integrity or Honesty is far more complex than just telling the truth. Research this term and compose a short paper outlining the ramifications of living with integrity.

12. In their attempt to live simply early Friends adopted a standard of plain dress. But sometimes their "sense of plainness" did not always jive with the purpose of living simply. Sometimes the "Quaker Gray" was not always plain. How well do Friends today hold to this testimony?

13. One would think that two-thousand years after Christ modeled the way of equality that humankind would have a good grasp of how equality may be done. What do you believe? Is equality a testimony strong among Friends these days? If not, how might this issue be addressed?

14. Are the three points about peace biblical? Can you compose a list of verses that support these three concepts?

15. If the mission statement for Friends as a whole is to gather people to Christ and to share in the spiritual needs of community what is your mission? Do you have a mission? Can you write out a personal mission statement?

16. Although Friends never lived communally like the Shakers did, community has always been important to Friends. In a short well-written essay describe your understanding of community and illustrate it by referencing your own experience as a member of a community. What role has community played in your spiritual formation?

17. Sometimes stewardship is conceived as simply wise use of one's funds but it goes well beyond just the use of one's resources. From a biblical perspective what is good stewardship? How do Friends churches today exhibit stewardship?

18. What are your thoughts on the historic Quaker belief that the outward forms of the sacraments (baptism and communion) are not sufficient for salvation? The Quaker belief in the sacramental universe is that all God's created universe is potentially a sacrament - a means through which we can commune with Christ. How have you experienced communion with Christ? Sacramental living is living in Christlikeness. When others see you, do they see the love of Christ?

19. An "eliminative adversative" is a contrastive conjunction which is used when one of the contrasts is negated in favor of the true choice. Do an exegetical study of the conjunction's use in these seven verses: Matthew 3:11, Luke 3:16, Mark 1:8, John 3:30, John 1:26, Acts 1:5, Acts 11:16.

20. Explain in a short essay how the Friends practice of communion is experienced in day-to-day living.

21. To explain the Quaker decision-making process the expression is used, "gathering a sense of the meeting," i.e. the decision makers sense God's desires, rather than their own, in the decisions to be made. How does this process differ from consensus?

22. Prepare a short research paper about the person and role of the Holy Spirit. How does the Holy Spirit give direction to your life?

23. Have you ever had to make an affirmation in a court of law? While everyone else was taking an oath were you uncomfortable being different by affirming instead? Did anyone question why you did this?

24. Demonstrations, vigils, marches, speeches—have you participated in any of these sorts of activities in order to promote peace? What is the best way to inform others of your interest in peacemaking?

25. Each Friends group has their own queries. Are you familiar with the queries from your meeting? How often have you pondered them? Do you have a set of queries of your own? How often do you ponder them?

26. The six queries given in the text are given as samples. Queries may contain much more specific detail than these. Collect and compare the queries of several Quaker bodies.

27. In a short essay relate the two concepts of the inward light and the act of worship.

28. Describe a time when you have experienced the Holy Spirit moving upon gathered Friends in such a way that the worship time was completely altered. Does this happen sufficiently today among Friends?

For Further Study

Anderson, Paul. *Following Jesus: The Heart of Faith and Practice.* Newberg: Barclay Press, 2013.

Ball, Charles. *Remembering Our Heritage: Studies in Friends Beliefs.* Whittier: California Yearly Meeting, 1973.

Barbour, Hugh and J. William Frost. *The Quakers.* Richmond: Friends United Press, 1994.

Barnett, Paul. *Why I am A Quaker.* Printed by the author, 1970.

Bates, Elias. *The Doctrine of Friends or Principles of the Christian Religion as Held by the Society of Friends Commonly Called Quakers.* Printed by the author, 1868.

Beals, Charles. *The Essential Baptism.* Richmond: Barclay Press, n.d.

Bevans, John. *A Brief View of the Doctrines of the Christian Religion as Professed by the Society of Friends.* Philadelphia: The Friends Bookstore, n.d.

Brinton, Howard. *Guide to Quaker Practice.* Wallingford: Pendle Hill, 1942.

Cooper, Wilmer. *A Living Faith; an Historical and Comparative Study of Quaker Beliefs.* 2nd Ed. Richmond: Friends United Press, 2006.

Foster, Richard J. *Celebration of Discipline: The Path to Spiritual Growth.* San Francisco: Harper San Francisco, 1998.

_____. *Freedom of Simplicity.* New York: Harper and Row, 1973.

Jones, Rufus. "Baptism and Communion." The American Friend Publishing Co., n.d.

_____. *The Faith and Practice of the Quakers.* Richmond: Friends United Press, n.d.

Kenworthy, Leonard. *Quakerism: A Study Guide on the Religious Society of Friends.* Dublin: Prinit Press, 1981.

Macy, Herman. *What About the Ordinances?* Newberg: Barclay Press, 1965.

Macy, Howard. *The Shalom of God.* Newberg: Barclay Press, 2018.

Roberts, Arthur. *The People Called Quakers.* Newberg: Oregon Yearly Meeting of Friends Churches Board of Publications, n.d.

Sims, Edgar. "The Baptism with the Holy Ghost: The Promise and Purpose." By the author, 1936.

_____. "Why Baptizest Thou?" By the author, n.d.

Vaughn, Delbert. *On Baptism and the Holy Spirit; in the Writings of the Early Church Pastors.* Houston: Enchiridion Publishing Company, 1980.

Willcuts, Jack. *Why Friends are Friends.* Newberg: Barclay Press, 1984.

Williams, Walter. *The Rich Heritage of Quakerism.* Newberg; Barclay Press, 1987.

Wilson, E. Raymond. *Uphill for Peace: Quaker Impact on Congress.* Richmond: Friends United Press, 1975.

Paul Anderson

Paul Anderson is Professor of Biblical and Quaker Studies at George Fox University and Adjunct Professor of New Testament Hermeneutics at Barclay College's School of Graduate Studies. He has a wonderful gift of teaching the Bible so that it lives as a dynamic witness to Jesus Christ.

Paul is the son of Alvin and Lucy Anderson, who taught at Barclay College. Paul's grandfather, Scott T. Clark, was the founding President of Barclay College. He was raised in Colombia, Ecuador, and Dominican Republic. Paul received his Ph.D. from Glasgow University.

Paul is internationally renowned for his scholarship in the New Testament, particularly the Johannine literature. He has written numerous books, including: *From Crisis to Christ: A Contextual Introduction to the New Testament, The Riddles of the Fourth Gospel,* and *The Christology of the Fourth Gospel.* Paul wrote the Commentary on John's Epistles in the *Baker Illustrated Bible Commentary.* His book, *Following Jesus: The Heart of Faith and Practice,* is a masterpiece of rich, practical resources to guide Christians of our generation in a contagious, life-transforming venture of following Jesus. Paul edited and wrote a new foreword to Elton Trueblood's *A Place to Stand*, and he wrote forewords to five of Henry Cadbury's books, including *George Fox's Book of Miracles.* Paul also wrote forewords to Rudolf Bultmann's *A Commentary on John* and four other books in the Johannine Monograph Series. He is currently writing the book, *Jesus in Johannine Perspective: A Fourth Quest for Jesus.* He is author of several other published books.

Among other editorial responsibilities, Paul edited *Evangelical Friend* for five years and *Quaker Religious Thought* for eleven years, and he is the founding editor of FAHE's Quakers and the Disciplines Series. He and Howard Macy edited *Truth's Bright Embrace: Essays and Poems in Honor of Arthur Roberts*, and he co-edited five volumes in the John, Jesus, and History Project.

A leader in the Friends Church, Paul is ecumenical in his vision and outlook. For example, he visited two Popes to share their mutual faith in Christ. He is a friend to all who know him, and a friend in the spirit of Jesus, who promised, "You are my friends if you do what I command you" (John 15:14). Paul and his wife, Carla, are the loving parents of three daughters: Sarah, Della, and Olivia.

FRIENDS TIMELINE

Events in the Friends Movement	World Events/Religious Literature
	4 B.C. – 590 A.D.: The Apostolic Church from the birth of Christ to the fall of Rome
	590 – 1517: The Medieval Church sees the expansion of power and influence of the Roman Catholic Church but also many reform-minded groups such as the Brethren of the Common life.
	1517: The Modern Church begins with the Reformation in Germany, Switzerland, Geneva, and England.
	1525: William Tyndale's New Testament translation
	1530: The Augsburg Confession
	1534: The Acts of Supremacy in England
	1536: Menno Simmons joins the Anabaptists and later leads the Mennonites.
	1541: John Knox leads reformation in Scotland.
	1559: Elizabethan Prayer Book published
1624: George Fox is born at Fenny Drayton in Leicestershire, England.	
	1642: The Civil War in England begins.
1643: Fox leaves home to become a stranger to all.	

1646: Fox realizes the need to know Christ.

1647: George Fox begins ministry in Mansfield and Nottinghamshire.

1650: The Blasphemy Act hits Quakers because of their belief in the Inner Light of Christ.

1650: Fox's first imprisonment

1652: Fox preaches at Firbank Fell beginning the Quaker movement.

1652: George Fox has vision at Pendle Hill.

1652: In June at Firbank Fell many begin to be added to the Quaker movement.

1654: The Valiant Sixty begin ministry.

1655: George Fox meets with Oliver Cromwell.

1657: Fox preaches in Wales and Scotland.

1657: The voyage of the Woodhouse (Robert Fowler)

1658: Mary Fisher travels to see the Sultan of Turkey.

1658: Quakers are banned from Plymouth Colony.

1646: Puritanism becomes the "official" religion in England.

1649: King Charles I is beheaded and the Commonwealth begins.

1653: The establishment of the Protectorate under Oliver Cromwell

1656: John Bunyan *Some Gospel Truths Opened*

1660: In England, the Restoration of the Monarchy with Charles II

Events in the Friends Movement	World Events/Religious Literature
	1661: The Clarendon Code strikes against all non-conformists.
	1662: The Act of Uniformity forcing the Anglican Book of Common Prayer on all people is passed.
1664: The Oath of Allegiance to the king is required of Quakers.	**1664:** The Conventicle Act disallows any groups of more than five to meet.
1666: The 5th Monarchy plot against Charles II is blamed on Quakers.	**1666:** John Bunyan, *Grace Abounding to the Chief of Sinners*
1671: George Fox makes a mission journey to North America.	**1669:** William Penn, *No Cross, No Crown*
1676: West Jersey established as Quaker colony	
1677: George Fox visits Holland and Germany.	
1681: Pennsylvania established as a Holy Experiment	**1678:** John Bunyan, *Pilgrim's Progress* (part 1)
1691: George Fox dies in London.	**1689:** The Toleration Act
	1695: John Locke, *The Reasonableness of Christianity*
1702: Quakers lose control of West Jersey.	
1715: Early Pennsylvania 'minute' against slavery	
	1730-1745: First Great Awakening
	1735: John Wesley, *Journal*

1741: Jonathon Edwards, "Sinners in the Hands of an Angry God"

1756: Friends withdraw from the Pennsylvania Assembly.

1758: Slave Trading is made illegal in Quaker colonies.

1761: London Yearly Meeting 'minute' against slave trading

1775: Pennsylvania Abolition Society founded

1775: the outbreak of the American Revolution

1776: the Declaration of Independence

1781: The Society of free Quakers is formed.

1787: Society for the Effecting of Abolition of the Slave

1789: The United States Constitution is adopted.

1789: The French Revolution

1790-1830: the Second Great Awakening

1795: Baltimore Yearly Meeting appoints an Indian Affairs Committee.

1812-1815: The War of 1812

1815: the end of the Napoleonic Wars

1815: Czar Alexander promotes Christian Alliance.

1827-1828: the Great Separation

1830: Joseph Smith founds the Church of Latter Day Saints.

1830-1840: the Charles G. Finney revivals

1833: Daniel Wheeler visits the South Pacific.

1845: the Wilbur/Gurney separations in New England

1846-1848: Mexican American War

Events in the Friends Movement	World Events/Religious Literature
1854: the Wilber/Gurney separations in Ohio	
	1859: Charles Darwin *Origin of the Species*
1861: Joel and Hannah Bean minister in the Sandwich Islands.	**1861-1865:** the American Civil War
1868: The Provisional Committee on Foreign Gospel Service (1865) becomes the Friends Foreign Mission Association in Britain.	
1869: Eli and Sybil Jones begin the mission school at Ramallah.	
1871: Samuel Purdie arrives in Mexico.	**1871:** Jehovah's Witnesses founded
	1871: Charles Darwin, *The Descent of Man*
1887: The Richmond Conference produces the Richmond Declaration of Faith.	
1892: A second conference of Orthodox Friends considers the pastoral system.	
1894: The American Friends Board of Foreign Missions is formed.	
1895: The Manchester Conference becomes a turning point for the Society in England.	
1897: A third American conference prepares a Unified Discipline.	
	1899-1902: the Boer War
1900: Hicksite Friends join together in the Friends General Conference.	
1902: A mission work is begun in East Africa.	

1902: The Five Years Meeting (which becomes the Friends United Meeting) is organized with all Yearly Meetings except Ohio and Philadelphia joining.

1914-1918: The Great War (WWI)

1917: The United States enters WWI.

1926: Central Yearly Meeting is established.1926 Oregon Yearly Meeting (now Northwest) leaves the Five Years Meeting.

1927: The Foreign Missionary Association and the Council of International Service join to become the Friends Service Council.

1937: A second World Conference of Friends, Swarthmore Pennsylvania is held.

1937: Kansas Yearly Meeting (now Mid-America) withdraws from the Five Years Meeting.

1937: The Friends World Committee for Consultation begins.

1939-1945: World War II

1949: the beginning of the Cold War

1950 -1952: the Korean War

1952: A Friends World Conference is held at Oxford, England.

1957: Rocky Mountain Yearly Meeting is formed.

1965: The Evangelical Friends Alliance is formed.

1966: The Five Years Meeting becomes Friends United Meeting.

1967: A Friends World Conference is held at Guilford College.

1967-1970: Nigerian Biafran War

Events in the Friends Movement	World Events/Religious Literature
1970: A conference at Saint Louis gathers Friends from all persuasions.	
1978: Evangelical Friends Mission (EFM) is founded.	
	1994: Rwandan genocide
2008: Evangelical Friends Church becomes Evangelical Friends International.	
2014: First National Friends Multiplication Conference is held at Barclay College.	

INDEX

ABOUT THE AUTHOR

Glenn Leppert was graduated with a B.A. degree from Northwest Nazarene University in Secondary Education (history and English). Before graduating he did a full year internship teaching English at a junior high school in Utah. Following graduation from college he and his wife, Sue, spent three years in a remote school in Nigeria as teachers (Glenn also served as principal) before returning to the states to do a M.A. in Religion from George Fox Evangelical Seminary. Glenn directed an inner-city education program for five years in the inner city of Portland, Oregon before becoming pastor of a Friends Church in Salem Oregon. While in Oregon, he was a counselor at a local elementary school and taught a large Child Evangelism release time class. He joined the faculty at Barclay College in 1985 and earned a M.A. in History from Fort Hays State University during his first two years at the college. He received a Ph.D. in History from Kansas State University in 2003 while continuing as full-time registrar and instructor.

He has written several textbooks that have been used in classes including one for Historical Books and a study guide for Romans. His favorite textbook is the current text for NT Greek classes at Barclay—*Using New Testament Greek*. He wrote the chapter on Barclay College for the book, *Founded by Friends*. He has presented several papers to various groups including the Kansas State History Teacher's Association and at the Eisenhower Library in Abilene, Kansas and People to People in Kansas City. He presented a paper on the Civil War at the Barclay College spring 2018 Colloquium and a paper on the transition from the Congress of the Confederation to the Congress of the United States in observance of Constitution day at the college.

Glenn Leppert

ABOUT THE CONTRIBUTOR

David W. Kingrey (D. Min.) is Professor of Theological and Biblical Studies and Director of the Master of Arts in Quaker Studies and Master of Arts in Spiritual Formation at Barclay College. He serves on the leadership team of Evangelical Friends Church – Mid America Yearly Meeting.

www.ingramcontent.com/pod-product-compliance
Lightning Source LLC
Chambersburg PA
CBHW021142090426
42740CB00008B/896